*Sally and her team are one of the friendlie:
have met. As an organisation they really fo
getting the most from that collective up-t
has been a great pleasure to work with them. Sally is an authority in the
property world, and her book is based on 25 years of experience in the
industry and is not to be missed.*

Nigel Risner, world-class motivational speaker

*If you are a landlord you need to buy this book and learn from Sally, the
most experienced person I know in this area.*

Simon Zutshi, author of property bestseller *Property Magic*

*Sally really does connect. Her passion and zeal for the subject, together
with an informative and authoritative approach, is not only stimulating but
refreshing. Highly commended.*

Mark Hayward, FNAEA (Honoured) FNAVA, Managing Director of the NAEA

*Sally is one of those super-energised people who love to keep landlords and
agents up-to-date with key issues which can occur when renting a property.
Sally is passionate about raising standards in the private rental sector and
helping landlords, agents and tenants have a positive and safe experience.*

Valerie Bannister, President of ARLA

*Sally Lawson is a very well-respected letting agent, business owner and
franchisor. A prolific commentator through social and traditional media on
the issues affecting the private rented sector, she is now vice president of
the Association of Residential Letting Agents (ARLA), has been recently
appointed to sit on the ARLA Board and represents the industry on several
high-profile working groups. With her fundamental knowledge and
understanding of the sector, this work will ensure that landlords fully
understand their rights and responsibilities towards their properties,
tenants and the public at large.*

David Cox, Managing Director of ARLA

*Sally is one of those people who eats, sleeps and breathes lettings
completely, in a way that most people warm to immediately. In the five
years I've known her, she has always been first in the queue to help
landlords and agents alike and her experience, coupled with her helpful
manner, is very refreshing. This book is a must for any landlord or property
investor.*

Nick Carlile, founder of Platinum Property Builder

I've got this Tenant ...

Everything a landlord should know
before buying a house!

SALLY LAWSON

THE CHOIR PRESS

First published in the United Kingdom in 2015 by
The Choir Press
www.ivegotthistenant.co.uk/lookinside/

ISBN 978-1-910864-05-0

Contents

CONTENTS

CONTENTS

Foreword

The private rented sector in the UK is growing faster than ever before. At the turn of the last century over 80% of people rented their properties from landlords. Due to successive Rent Acts and rent control, the introduction of social housing, and the massive increase in the percentage of the population owning their own home, by 1990 the sector had shrunk to its smallest in recorded history.

However, with regulatory liberalisation and the introduction of 'no-fault' possession under Section 21 of the Housing Act 1988, combined with fiscal modernisation and the creation of the buy-to-let mortgage in 1996, the market began to recover.

Today, the private rented sector comprises around 20% of all properties in the UK and this trend is set to continue as rising house prices mean that many may never be able to save enough deposit or secure sufficient mortgage finance to own their own home. It is therefore more imperative than ever that landlords provide good-quality and well-managed accommodation.

There is a general myth that investing in property is easy. You put an offer on a property, take out a buy-to-let mortgage, get some tenants and off you go. If only it were that simple.

Rental yields are not all they are believed to be and landlords can no longer bank on capital appreciation alone. Remember that we are in a period of historically low interest rates. Many will forget that the Bank of England base rate was over 10% less than 20 years ago and therefore landlords, who are managing a business, need to plan for interest rate rises or risk losing what is probably not only their largest investment after the property in which they live, but also their tenant's home.

There are over 100 Acts of Parliament and numerous sets of regulations that govern the private rented sector. From property conditions and the number of toilets and sinks needed in a property through to managing tenants' money, energy perform-ance certificates, gas safety checks, tenancy agreements, taxation and now immigration checks, almost every aspect of letting a property is in some way regulated. And there is undoubtedly more to come.

Therefore, from legal requirements to best practice advice, it is more important than ever that landlords and letting agents can access all the necessary information in one place, especially with more legislation now governing the private rented sector than ever before.

Sally Lawson is a very well-respected letting agent, business owner and franchisor. A prolific commentator through social and traditional media on the issues affecting the private rented sector, she is vice president of the Association of Residential Letting Agents (ARLA), has been recently appointed to sit on the ARLA Board and represents the industry on several high-profile working groups. With her fundamental knowledge and understanding of the sector, this work will ensure that landlords fully understand their rights and responsibilities towards their properties, tenants and the public at large.

David Cox
Managing Director
Association of Residential Letting Agents (ARLA)

Introduction

When venturing into the world of becoming a landlord there are so many things that you need to know, so many laws you need to abide by and rules you can very easily break.

Many landlords think property management is simply collecting rent and sorting out maintenance on the property, but it is so much more far-reaching than this.

I have been in property since 1990, owning and running an extremely successful lettings business, and during that time I have let and managed over 6,000 properties and tenancies and yet I am still learning continuously. You see, the law is always changing; new test cases going to court change the rules by which we as landlords have to abide and therefore you can never sit still.

I have run a letting agency, helped others to set up letting agency businesses as a franchisor, built up and run my own property portfolio for the last two decades, and taught the subject of tenancy law to thousands of staff and delegates over the years. This has given me a great multi-dimensional view on the property industry from all angles.

As a landlord I understand the desire to keep the 'property-letting' side of the business easy and hassle-free as well as profitable, the desire not to spend too much so as not to eat into your profit as well as wanting great tenants who will treat your properties as their own. As an investor I understand the importance of the numbers; the property has got to 'stack up' or else it is not worth the risk or hassle. I have bought and refurbished/furnished over 430 properties to create the 'ideal' letting unit, using the benefit of my years in the lettings game and my knowledge of what tenants want from tens of thousands of tenant viewings conducted.

As a letting agent I have had the great pleasure of working with thousands of landlords from all walks of life. I have helped them go from property novices to large portfolio investors and have taken them through the emotional hurdles and fears. This has been hugely rewarding, and I am pleased to say that, contrary to the news, most landlords are good, honest, hard-working people who want to do the right thing; they just need to be educated in how to do so. It disheartens me that so many agents are scared to tell landlords what they need to know or do, or maybe they do not know themselves.

As you can imagine, over the years landlords have asked me tens of thousands of questions about what to do or not to do and their fears about the lettings industry. I have walked them through their first 'non-paying tenant', property damage and legal disputes, and have accompanied hundreds to court to help them defend themselves or repossess their property. Many landlords come to this industry uneducated in what the require-ments of a landlord are, but if they are conscientious and caring they generally make very good landlords. However, some should never be landlords at all.

As a letting agent you get to see both sides of the story, too; you might have the tenant crying on the phone because they have no heating in the middle of winter and a small baby to keep warm, and the landlord on the other line wanting a week to obtain three quotes. As an agent you are employed by the landlord, but you also have a 'duty of care' to the tenant. If you do not look after the tenant as the law dictates then the landlord could also be liable to prosecution from the tenant or council. It is sometimes an agent's role to deliver news the landlord does not want to hear but needs to know in order to protect himself and his tenant: a difficult place to sit.

As a business owner, franchisor and trainer it has been my task to educate my staff, taking them through the NFoPP Lettings and Management qualifications (which I do with my team through in-house training courses I developed), and to train franchise owners to be great letting agents, running successful businesses. I have also acted as a mentor and consultant working with many other letting agents and property investors, helping them to create the 'correct' processes, systems and knowledge to run their business.

As a board member of ARLA (the Association of Residential Letting Agents) and vice president I find myself at the sharp end of legislation changes and proposals, sometimes battling with government or local councillors on hot topics. Therefore I have to keep abreast of the law, which is a moving target and quite time-consuming.

I speak at events all across the country and over the years have given thousands of delegates my educational and thought-provoking presentation on lettings, filled with little anecdotes and example scenarios I have come across throughout the years. I have taught lettings laws and regulations to many educational organisations. I have been a regular guest speaker on BBC Radio WM, and at the time of writing I am the Midlands media spokesperson for ARLA.

Training has taught me one thing: that you don't know what you don't know!

This is so true in the case of landlords. I have landlords with over 70 properties who do not know the really basic stuff like what notices to serve to get a tenant out. I have met landlords with over 300 units who are operating completely illegally, with no gas certification and performing illegal evictions daily! The scary thing is they were blissfully ignorant and thought they were doing everything right. Some were actually training others.

The private rented sector has now overtaken social housing in the provision of homes in the UK and has been predicted to grow to as high as 50% of the total housing stock by 2050, due to the councils' non-investment in new council housing and the difficulty faced by the younger generation in buying their own homes now.

With this in mind we as private landlords have a massive part to play in the future housing of the population, and that is a responsibility that needs to be taken seriously. The government is starting to realise this and really focusing on the PRS (Private Rented Sector) market, with additional licensing and regulation. I'm sure much more will be imposed upon us over the next few years to improve standards, in order to protect tenants and the population.

So my mission is to educate the poor landlord and tell him all the things that he doesn't know so that he does know them and can then make a choice to do something about them. If he is a good landlord he will do so and will be rewarded by happier tenants, longer-staying tenants have better agents working for him (if he chooses), better and higher rents, better returns and better quality of properties too. And if I can do that in a book that is easy to read and understand, then I have achieved my mission.

This book is not an exhaustive guide, but it will tell you all the things you need to know. If you want to know more about any of those things then you will be able to look deeper, knowing what you are looking for.

By the time you have finished this book, you will know more than most other landlords you will ever meet, so please spread the word. Let's clean up the reputation of the landlord. We're not bad people; we just need more access to information.

Managing Your Properties

Are you managing your portfolio or is it managing you?

This chapter will cover some of the most common mistakes landlords make over and over again.

How to get your property let fast and minimise those voids!

Buy to suit your personality

Minimising your voids starts with doing your research and buying the right property that will rent well in the market that *you* want to be in. Many landlords make mistakes here and find their lives very stressful and unhappy and suffer huge voids continually, but with a bit of research all these headaches can be avoided.

Over the years I have met so many landlords who decided to invest in property because they wanted a 'passive' income. They imagine still doing the day job (or eventually giving that up) and having lots of fun living on the money that the property generates. Unfortunately this is not generally the case. I have met landlords with 450 units, 250 units, 150 units, who confess their life is a mess, no time for themselves, the phone constantly going, staff running around not knowing what they are doing, the councils and government bodies like the planning office continually on their case, high arrears rates and near-bankruptcy! How can this be? They should be living the dream!

The key is to look at your personality. What type of person are you, and what type of landlord do you want to be? Do you see yourself going round on a Friday night with the rent books chasing tenants for their rent, dealing with drug dealers and asylum seekers on a daily basis? If so then this might be the strategy for you! Be warned, though: most letting agents won't deal with this type of tenancy, so you may well be on your own here. If, however, you prefer a hands-off type of investment, you just want a nice family to look after your investment and not give you much hassle, then you need to reconsider. Where would your ideal tenant want to live?

Research the market

Once you have identified the sort of market you want to enter, you need to look at the cash you have available, and buy the right sort of property that matches your end-goal tenants with the best return. For example, if you want to deal with middle-class working tenants but don't have a lot of cash, look to a flat in a better area. Or if you have a good amount of cash available but want a higher cash flow return, and still want to deal with the better tenants, then you could consider a professional house share: buying a larger property in a better area and converting it into a quality house share for professional people will tradition-ally give you higher returns.

But whatever you do, buy to suit you. A lot of the stress comes from being in the wrong market and your life taking a wrong turn down a path you don't want to travel.

So once you have figured out what market you want to enter in the buy-to-let arena, you then need to research and take advice. The absolutely number-one thing you must get right from the start is buying the right property. I know it sounds obvious, but so many landlords buy property for completely wrong reasons and then spend years suffering the consequences of it.

If you are going to buy a property to rent then take advice from people in the know (and be careful whose advice you buy!), but make sure you are buying a property that *will rent* and rent quickly to the right type of tenant, over and over again! For this letting agents are a great source of knowledge, but choose one with a long history of experience, preferably through good and bad markets.

By now you should have identified your target market and price range. Start by looking online to see which letting agents work in that target market. Call them up and tell them what you want to do. Have some key questions ready, like ...

- 'What type of property would best suit X type of client?'

- 'Where would you buy if you had £Xk available?'

- 'Where should I absolutely avoid?'

- 'Do you know if the blocks of flats in that area have any lease restrictions preventing letting?'

- 'What property lets the quickest in that area: a detached, a semi, one with a particular number of rooms?'

- 'What's the student/DSS/professional let market like at the moment in this area?'

- 'Where do you find most of the tenants come from? Are there any major employers I should be buying close to?'

- 'Do you run a buy-to-let advisory service?'

If they run a landlord's advisory service you can really work with them and they will then support you through the decision stage of property purchase. Make sure you ascertain the level of experience of the person offering the advice, though, as you want someone who has been in the industry a while and seen the highs and lows over the good and bad markets for property.

Property portals such as Rightmove,[1] Mouseprice[2] and Zoopla[3] are a great source of information on how much properties are on the market for. If I am offered a property in an area I do not know, my first port of call for a rental assessment is these sites.

I was offered seven flats in a block in central Birmingham two years ago at an alleged 'absolute bargain'. I was told (by a solicitor) that the flats were worth £170k but I could buy them at £110k, and that they would fetch a market rent of £750pcm. *Wow,* I thought, *let's have a look.* Within ten minutes I found out the truth. There were 27 flats available for sale in this block for prices ranging from £80k to £140k and the penthouse at £190k; there were 46 available to rent at the moment with rents ranging from £450pcm to £750pcm. With this volume of properties available for both sale and rent, there was no way I would ever achieve the figures quoted, as the cheapest ones would generally let or sell first. A very valuable ten minutes, I would say! Don't believe what people tell you or what you read; check it out for yourself.

If I had found that the figures stacked up, I would have then started calling letting agents in the area to check out the facts before taking the time to view the flats.

---

[1] http://www.rightmove.co.uk
[2] http://www.mouseprice.com
[3] http://www.zoopla.co.uk

If you buy a flat with over 40 others available to rent at the same time you are asking for trouble, until the market there settles down.

Many would-be landlords make the mistake of taking advice from estate agents and end up buying a property purely because 'it was a really good price and I couldn't turn it down', but it's in the worst street, in the worst part of town and will only be attractive to the worst kind of tenant! This will lead to large voids and troublesome management as the property keeps getting trashed, leading to high refurbishment and maintenance costs! But it was a great price ... or was it? Remember, estate agents want to sell you a house; they are *not* the ones to take advice from.

There are so many websites now that you can use to see the value of properties sold, like Zoopla and Mouseprice, so there is no excuse for ever buying an overvalued property.

Location, location, location

You have heard it all before, but it is so true. There can be 'wrong ends of a street' which, if you're not in the know, you can fall into the trap of. Use your eyes, look around the street; what does it look like? Is there a 'family from hell' next door or nearby? If so, move on; there will be plenty more.

One thing that has puzzled me for years is the number of landlords prepared to buy properties without ever seeing them or apparently doing *any* research!

Quite often they see a property offered and it looks lovely in the picture, a sweet two-bed semi in a modern little cul-de-sac, just on the edge of town. What the picture doesn't tell you is that to get to it, you have to drive through the roughest council estate within a 50-mile radius, and all the windows are boarded up on the street leading to this lovely little quiet cul-de-sac because even the council can't find tenants for it.

What this means is that any tenant that gets lured in by the photo will more often than not just drive on and not stop to carry out the viewing, fearing for their own safety, so you end up with, yet again, the wrong tenant or no tenant. I have seen this over and over again.

Visit the property, check out the location, ask advice from numerous sources and be sure before you buy. These types of properties are cheap for a reason!

A property is only worth what someone is prepared to pay!

Many, many landlords get far too hung up on 'my property is worth £X'. I'm afraid it is only worth what someone is prepared to pay for it. It doesn't matter who told you what, or what the top price on Rightmove is; you have to look at what people are paying.

Beware of common traps here.

A typical example of this is new builds. If you were to ask me at the time of writing what a new centrally-located two-bed flat with en-suite, overlooking the canal, would fetch in my town, I would be able to tell you, 'Around £595pcm furnished,' and I would not be wrong (based on the very limited information given).

If a landlord were then to go and buy a brand new two-bed flat in the new canal-side development just down the road, where there are 240 coming available next week, then would he get that price? No.

Why? Because there are 240 other flats available. This creates its own 'sub-market' and survival of the cheapest and best-fitted-out begins. Desperate landlords who have stretched themselves will drop the rent to, say, £450 to get their flats let fast, and they will normally let first; other landlords will recognise the competition and go to town putting in flat-screen TVs, leather-framed beds etc., and they will probably achieve around the £595pcm (if theirs is the best), but the rest? They will get let eventually when they become the cheapest or the best available, so be careful of mass 'sub-markets' and ensure you are at the top on presentation or the bottom on price.

A great thing to do if investing in new builds such as this is to allow yourself a 'start-up' budget: leave some money in the bank and just drop the rent right down to get it let fast for the first eighteen months to two years, and then edge the rent back up to a market rental figure. When all the flats are rented out the rents will stabilise as they will all be coming available at different times and your normal market rent can be achieved.

A word of warning, though. If you buy in a town where there is lots and lots of building taking place there could be a 'master sub-market' going on, not just in your block but with regard to, say, two-bed flats in the city as a whole. These situations are much harder to overcome and will take a lot longer to recover.

Occupancy is king

This is so true. An empty property costs you money (you have nothing coming in at all, you will end up maintaining the place, paying council tax etc.), so don't get precious over achieving the 'market rent'; take what someone is prepared to pay. With my properties I always try to set the rent just below the market rent, so they get filled quickly, and I very rarely increase the rent as I like to keep my tenants in occupation. I know that a good tenant is worth keeping.

Presentation

We have already discussed how this is so important for getting your property let in a sub-market, but remember that, whatever property you have, you are part of the 'lettings market' in general at all times and always have competition. With property websites now it is so easy to see both external and internal photos of other landlords' properties; have a look and see what they are doing. Remember that if they are being advertised they have not been let, so they will not all have it right, but taking a look will give you an idea of what you are up against.

Having conducted thousands and thousands of viewings with tenants, I am pretty aware of tenants' likes and dislikes. A few things to look out for are:

- Décor. This should be neutral. Tenants will all have different tastes, so keep colours to a minimum and keep the décor clean and free of marks. This will help with your inventory, too.

- Showers. If you have to choose between a shower and a bath, go for the shower; it's quicker, cleaner and cheaper. Baths only are a real no-no for sharers!

- Gardens. Smaller is better; gardens are a hindrance to tenants and they will only do the minimum. If you have a large garden, hire a gardener.

- Parking. Lack of parking can be a real issue nowadays, except in certain city centres like London.

- Dirt. No one likes to live with someone else's dirt. Get the place cleaned before every tenancy.

- Heating. This is one of the key requirements and you can be forced to carry out additional heating work by the council through the HHSRS (Housing Health and Safety Rating System) if you do not provide adequate heating for the accommodation.

- Damp. This is a definite no. Again this can result in enforced work through the HHSRS, if the tenant reports you, so get it sorted.

- Furnished or unfurnished. This varies depending on your location. In my home town, if it is two beds or less it has to be furnished to let; if it is three beds or more, unfurnished is best. The worst option? Part-furnished. So you're looking for someone who has a sofa but not a bed, has a fridge but not a washing machine! A real nightmare! In London furniture packs can be rented, therefore most tenants will want unfurnished so that they can choose their furniture to suit them. These are generally not cost-effective outside London as they can cost more than the rent, so they're not available.

So here I would picture your ideal tenant, research your competition, speak to the local letting agents and get their advice, and then design your furniture and décor plan to suit your ideal tenant. For example, in one of my properties, which is a former hotel converted into flats, I like to have 'mature' tenants rather than youngsters. Now, I can't really advertise 'mature people wanted', so I designed the presentation to suit the tenants I want. I have top-quality slightly patterned carpets, neutral décor, solid good-quality wooden furniture, well-designed kitchens and comfortable bedrooms with plenty of storage, a communal garden and a storage shed each, and it all has to be impeccably clean with mark-free décor. If I were aiming at the younger market, then I would have all leather and chrome with a minimalist feel.

By doing this I have avoided any issues with noise, parties etc. and my tenants stay for longer periods than we would normally expect.

Marketing your property

So you have identified your target market, done your research, taken advice and checked out the competition. You have then bought the property that most suits your goals, and now it's time to get it let! How do you do that?
Marketing again is different dependent on the type of market you want to aim at and, to a lesser degree, your area. Not all properties are the same.

Advertising for students

If you have identified that 'students' are the market you want to aim for, then you need to be on the universities' lists of landlords, Gumtree, rent-aroom, spareroom.com student lets etc. Have a board in the window saying 'student accommodation' and postcards out in all the local newsagents and shops advertising your rooms to let.

LHA (Local Housing Authority) tenants

Similar to the students: advertise with leaflets through the LHA-let areas and council estates, Gumtree, the free newspapers, postcards in the betting shops and fast food joints etc., but also on the property portals Zoopla and Rightmove.

Professional lets

The marketing for professional lets is rather different. Your prospective tenants are more likely to use the internet to house-search in their lunch break at work or at the weekends. In my company over 99% of our tenant enquiries come from property portals. So you really need to be on Rightmove and other property portals for this type of tenant. Of course you can try all the other mediums, but we have found time and time again that this is what creates the best results. The newspaper used to be really effective, but the internet has very much taken over from the paper now, and generally it is now more the lower-earning brackets that will rely on the newspaper.

So how do you get on Rightmove? Landlords can't advertise directly through Rightmove, but many letting agents will be able to put your property on the website. It's not as easy as it sounds, though. Property portals have a huge number of properties on them and your property is just one amongst many, so you will need to stand out. Photos are very important and what we said about the presentation, cleanliness, tidiness and furnishings (if applicable) will become of paramount importance here!

Photos

Do not take photos of a half-finished, untidy, undecorated, messy house with gardens overgrown and then wonder why you have had no enquiries. You have got to get the work done quickly. If it's halfway through just take the outside picture, but get the inside ones ASAP.

Because of the volume of properties available to rent on these sites, tenants viewing them will scan through the lists quite quickly and they will either stop at yours or not based on the image they see, so this needs to be really good! Choose a sunny day, good angle and good distance but not too far away; make sure the lawn is cut and the garden tidy, windows clean and no cars obstructing the view. Have a look on the property sites and see which properties catch your eye and which ones don't!

Once your property has caught someone's eye on a website, you want them to look into it further or 'click through' to the particulars. Your 'click-through rate' – the percentage of people who click on your property after seeing it – will singlehandedly determine the success of your properties on the property portal and the number of enquiries you receive. To get people to 'click through' you will need internal pictures to show as the property portal will say '(7 more images)' to encourage prospective tenants to look further. So you need to get those quality internal pictures on as soon as possible.

Pay real attention to the detail here. An unmade bed will look awful and uninviting; a cluttered kitchen will look messy, as will a bathroom with bottles everywhere. De-clutter, dress up beds, cut the lawn, remove shower bottles; make the place look as clutter-free and organised and clean as it possibly can.

Descriptions

Once you have lured them in with the photos, the descriptions will be the next thing a potential tenant will look at, and it is these that will encourage a tenant to enquire about a viewing. You need a really long description for people to see when they 'click through', but remember that when they are looking at their search list of lots of properties they will only see the first few lines, so always make sure that you mention the key points first: 'two weeks rent-free', 'next to Hammersmith tube station', 'available now'. This will ensure any special features catch the searcher's eyes.

The description must mention all the details about the property: how many bedrooms, kitchens and bathrooms, shower or bath, en-suites, the size of the garden, parking facilities, furnishings, heating provided, when the property is available and any special offers. Don't lie. It has to be truthful and factual. If the property is small, say 'compact'; don't say 'spacious'. By being completely factual and getting everything in the description you will reduce the amount of time you will waste doing useless viewings, with people saying, 'But I thought it was a ground-floor flat'; 'Oh, I didn't realise it was furnished'; 'It's not as big as it looks in the photos.' In a way the description should pre-empt the enquiries you get through.

Agents

Many 'professional' tenants will want the security of renting through a letting agent; in their mind this gives them protection from unscrupulous landlords and protects their deposits. If you are choosing an agent to market your property, I would do your research on their marketing ability. With all the knowledge you have just learnt here, you now know what their properties should look like on their chosen property portal, so have a look! If you find that there are hardly any photos, that the pictures are blurred, that they do not take internal pictures, you have an idea as to their skill at marketing. Before speaking to any agent about marketing I would always check out this free skill checker; it's so obvious and readily available to all of us.

I would ask them what their click-through rate is. They will also be given a ranking from Rightmove against the other agents in the town, for example first out of five or fifth out of five. Guess which one's list you want to be on. A simple check that can really make a huge difference.

So you've checked out your agents and you're convinced you have selected the one most adept at marketing your property in your chosen market, but there is one last vitally important check you need to make to ensure that they are good at marketing. If an agent has lots of beautifully photographed and detailed properties on their books, there is one other thing they need to let the property: tenants.

Many agents, much to my surprise, do not take down tenants' details! Why, oh, why? I don't understand it; they spend thousands and thousands marketing themselves and their properties, and when the prospective tenants call, unless they actually ask for a viewing, they can't be bothered to take down their details. This is one to watch.

The best way to measure their success in this market is to get on the phone to them and be a tenant. Ask for something you know they haven't got and see if they ask for your information; if they don't, move on. This shows lack of staff training and management or poor systems. You might want to give them the benefit of the doubt and ring a few times, but it's a very worthwhile exercise.

Re-marketing

If you use an agent and they then manage the let, when your property comes available again, it is worth checking the property portal to see if your property is advertised, make sure they are satisfactorily re-marketing your property and ask for updated photos or descriptions if needed.

How to make the paperwork work for you

If you have the right paperwork, this is your defence in the event of anything going wrong. If every tenant were honest, respected the property, paid the rent and acted exactly as we wanted them to act, then there would never be any need for paperwork. Unfortunately this is not always the case.

When a tenant fails to do what we want them to do – when they don't look after the property as they should do, have unknown people move in with them, don't pay the rent, damage the property or just run off without paying – it is the tenancy agreement and the associated documents to which you will turn to get recompensed.

With a good tenancy, both parties will understand exactly what is expected of them at all times. The agreement will be clearly written and easy to understand and will include any particular 'special clauses' there are for that particular tenancy: for example, 'the tenant is allowed to keep one house-trained cat on the premises but no other pets', which is quite clear and specific.

Tenancy agreements by nature are generally quite vague as they are written to suit all circumstances. A good tenancy agreement is one that has been extended to cover all the odd little nuances that come along over the years.

Be wary of using the same agreement for years, too. Tenancy law is changing all the time as new test cases come and go, and therefore you have to ensure you are always using an up-to-date agreement.

There are also different types of tenancy agreements which I will cover later in the legal section. Always check to make sure you are using the correct agreement. Tenancy law is rather odd in that, even if you use the wrong agreement, within law the tenant still has all the rights of the agreement they are in fact eligible for (the agreement you should have used, that is), so you may not have agreed on what you think you have.

An example of this is where you have used a licence agreement and not an assured shorthold tenancy; your tenant's situation, however, dictates that you should have used an assured shorthold tenancy agreement. This means that in the eyes of the law the tenant does actually have all the protection of the AST. If you were to repossess the property using the methods required under a licence agreement, therefore, you would in fact be performing an illegal eviction, and this carries huge penalties if prosecuted. So be very careful here. There is a tenancy flowchart later in this book to check which agreement you should be using.[4]

---

[4]   Under the subheading 'Which contracts should you use?' in the chapter on law.

Also within tenancy law there are certain guidelines laid down as to how you must treat a tenant, and what rights you and they have. Even if the agreement says otherwise these rights must be adhered to, so be careful.

Inventory

This is now a very important document. In the absence of a well-drawn-up inventory it is unlikely you will be able to withhold money from a tenant's deposit for damage to your property. This is not something to risk. You must ensure that your inventory consists of all items in the property and then gives the location and condition of each item, listing any marks or damage. You must also refer to the keys, meter readings and garden.

The items that generally get missed off inventories are the 'fixed' items. Many landlords feel that it is not worth writing down the radiators, the colour of the walls, the doors and their handles etc., but they could not be more wrong.

One landlord I went to see a few years ago had rented a flat to a young chap and had not bothered to write down such stuff; instead he had just listed all the loose items in the flat. When I went to see him after he got his keys back, it was the first time he had been in the flat since the tenant had moved out.

The ex tenant had painted the entire flat in black gloss! The walls, ceiling, storage heaters, woodwork, uPVC window frames: the lot. The guy was fighting back the tears when I walked in. How awful. But because he had not made a note of the colour of the flat or the décor, he would have had little chance of being compensated through the tenant's deposit, although I'm sure he tried!

There have also been stories of boilers and radiators being taken from properties. In one of my properties (which I had rented to family, and that's another story), I found them trying to remove the log burner! I have known of copper piping and lead flashing being stolen by departing tenants, too, so write everything down.

When you have made a log of everything including its location, colour and condition, get the tenant to sign a copy of the inventory upon moving in. That way you have written agreement that that was the condition of the property when they moved in.

There are courses you can go on to improve your inventory-writing skills, and there is actually a qualification and a recognised body for inventory professionals. The organisation is called APIP, the Association of Professional Inventory Providers, and its courses are available through NFoPP, but there are many professional inventory preparation companies around too, if you are not letting through an agent.

Gas certificates

Most people know that you have to get a gas certificate, but so many people still get this horribly wrong. Some landlords I worked with, when I first met them, had 'not got around' to doing their gas certificates and literally had hundreds expired. Sometimes gas certificate renewal had been delegated to staff and they had not felt it important and, again, had not got around to it.

The gas safety rules carry a penalty of £5,000 or six months in jail or both, for each offence, so that can be quite hefty with over 100 properties!

In brief, as I will cover this in much more detail in the legal section of this book, you must ensure you have a gas safety certificate saying the property is safe, created by a suitably qualified Gas Safe engineer BEFORE the tenant moves in. You must also give EACH TENANT a copy of the gas certificate before they move in.

You must ensure that the renewal date is logged somewhere to remind you to get the renewals done on time, in order to prevent there being any period where there is no valid gas certificate. Any renewed gas certificates must be sent to the tenant within 28 days of being completed.

Also you must make records of any gas works done and who did them, and you must keep these records for two years. I will cover this more later.

Standing order

This is one of the most efficient ways to collect your rent. Set up a standing order for the rent to be paid into your accounts, make a note of when you expect to receive the rent and then you can chase it if it does not come in on time.

Setting up a standing order is free and easy. Remember to put references on your standing orders, though, as when you have a few properties, you will not know what money has come in from where!

How to get better tenants, and avoid the bad ones!

Guarantors

Some landlords go on gut instinct and I have heard many stories saying that this works, but I like to see hard proof before I trust my or any of my staff's 'instinct'. This is because some tenants have mastered the art of appearing wonderful, professional and the perfect tenant. A month or so later all is revealed: the rent is late, they are not really working, there are twice as many people living in the property as there should be and the lounge houses a menagerie of animals. We then have a lot of explaining to do, and we will fall back on the paperwork and the referencing done at the outset.

You need to set yourself a list of criteria for your tenant, and stick to it. Be strict with yourself when faced with a lovely tenant who doesn't quite stack up, and have 'what if' measures.

We would all love tenants who have been in their job three years, earn 40 times the rent and are UK residents with three years' worth of references from landlords, but sometimes people don't fit that mould, so what do you do?

Ask for a guarantor. These are so useful. When anything doesn't quite stack up – when they don't quite earn enough, haven't quite been in the country for 12 months etc. – we ask for a guarantor. This is a great way of ascertaining whether the tenant is trustable or not. Someone who knows them infinitely better than you is not going to put their name to paper, committing to pay the rent in the case of a default, if they know that the tenant is bad news.

Careful, though: you need to reference the guarantor in the same way as the tenant. You want the guarantor to be a UK-living homeowner and they must sign the guarantor's paperwork too, so there is some extra work required here. They also need to be made aware of what they are signing and what they are committed to.

I've always found though that with a good home-owning guarantor, if your tenant goes into arrears, you are a lot more likely to receive your rent.

Landlords' references

So many people ask for landlords' references, and this is good as a tenant's former landlord will or should give you a good insight into what the tenant is like, but here is a question for you ...

Imagine you had the tenant from hell living in your property and you were trying to get rid of them. If you then got a call from another landlord asking you for a reference for your tenant, who had applied for their property and said they wanted to move in next week ... what would you say?

That is why you must always go to the landlord *before* the previous landlord to get a reference. They will tell you the truth. You could even look to the landlord before that! Keep digging. A bad tenant is a bad tenant and they usually leave a string of disgruntled landlords behind them.

Credit check

This is a must. You need the tenant's consent and signature of authority to do a credit search. You can then credit-search them using one of the credit referencing agencies available. These will give you lots of useful information: any county court judgements, bankruptcies, alias addresses, the dates they have registered on the voters' roll (or not).

Very, very useful tools. We search their alias addresses as well to make sure that if there are any skeletons hidden in the cupboard or they have tried to pretend they have lived somewhere that they haven't, we will find out.

If your prospective tenant is a limited company you can also perform company searches to ascertain their time trading, directorships, net worth and any charges, borrowings or bad debts. DueDil[5] is a good place to start for this.

Employment references

These are extremely valuable. We tend to go back three years. You are looking for someone who has spent at least the last full year in full-time employment without any breaks.

Make sure that NO reference you take is a mobile number. We have had ladies of the night claiming to be accountants, giving out their friends' mobile numbers as employers' references. You want a landline, a business name and, if possible, a fax number to fax the reference to and get a signed copy faxed back. Google the number and company, too, to see what this brings up.

You are asking when the tenant started, what job they do, whether it is full-time and permanent, and what salary they are on.

---

[5] http://www.duedil.com

National Insurance number

We always take this as if the tenant defaults and you need to chase them for arrears there are a few things you can do with the NI number, including getting an attachment to earnings to recover your arrears from.

Next of kin

This one works beautifully. You need the next of kin in case the tenant is hurt and you need to contact their nearest relative. But this is also extremely useful if you lose your tenant!

Imagine your tenant has run off and you have arrears and you can't trace him; he is ignoring you. You call Auntie Flo and ask for little Jimmy. She says, 'Oh, he's coming around for tea tomorrow at 6pm; why don't you call then?' It works a dream.

You must not hassle Auntie Flo, but she can be really useful, and the fact that you have rung her will make Jimmy realise he cannot hide from the problem and will generally get him to do something.

How to manage those arrears

If you have bought the right property in the right location, you have referenced your tenants fully and you have followed the guidelines in this book, then your chances of getting a 'bad tenant' have already substantially decreased. But sometimes people will just generally hit hard times; some will play the game.

You must have a 'process' for handling rent arrears. It is actually a defence in court against allegations of harassment if you can demonstrate that you have always carried out such a process, so work out a process that suits you.

Below is the system that we use for chasing rent arrears. We have less than 2% of the rent we are owed overdue at the time of writing, so this process works. You have to stick to the system, though, without fail. You cannot bend. A process is a process that is followed for everyone.

Added security

As we advised earlier, you should always try to get guarantors for any applications that look a little weak. If the tenant does not have a guarantor, six months' rent in advance on a six-month contract should do it!

When you have an account that falls into arrears and you have a guarantor, you must keep the guarantor informed the whole way, just as though they were the tenant. So whenever you write to or call the tenant, you do the same with the guarantor.

Most tenancy agreements demand that the rent be paid in advance and specify that it is the tenant's obligation to get the rent to you, not for you to collect it, so I am assuming this is the case here.

Week One arrears

As soon as the monthly rent is noted to be late, this is when the tenant is technically in arrears. Our system flags up the situation after seven days of the money not coming in, so you need a system that will alert you or remind you in the same way. At this point you give the tenant a call or write to them with a friendly letter, saying something along the lines of, 'It appears something may have gone wrong; could you have a look at it and forward the rent or notify us if there is a problem?'

You can't beat a phone call to get the tenant into action and to quickly find out what they are saying is the problem. However, you need something in writing.

Week Two arrears

Fourteen days after the first missed rental payment, the second letter and phone call are due to find out the problem. The tenant has not responded to your first call/letter or has not stuck to the arrangement set, so this time you need to be firmer.

This letter needs to be worded a bit stronger and refer to the previous letter. It could say something like, 'I am deeply concerned, following our previous conversation and letter, that still no rent has been paid. If no rent is paid in the next seven days I will prepare to start court action against you.'

Week Three arrears

This is effectively the final letter. Here you tell the tenant that despite your efforts, they have not responded and you are now left with no option but to take action through the courts to repossess the property. Explain that they will receive no further letters from you and if no payment is received in the next few days legal action will commence. Follow up again with a phone call, reiterating this.

Week Four arrears

The tenant is now effectively two months in arrears and on a monthly assured shorthold tenancy you now have a right to repossess the property through the courts, as long as all your paperwork is above-board and correct.

At this point you will prepare a Section 8 notice citing grounds 8, 10 and 11, which need to be worded in full, and send this to the tenant.

This notice tells the tenant that you will be starting court action in 14 days.

You allow two days for service (16 days total), and then you commence legal action through the courts.

Warning! Do not harass

There is no reason to be unpleasant, nasty, angry etc. even though you might want to be. You must aim to be calm and professional at all times. Do not harass the tenant at work or by telling their boss or their family, as the penalties for harassment are pretty severe for landlords. You must also not be tempted to cut off services to the premises, and you still have a duty to maintain the property as you would if they were paying the rent. So be careful; any un-landlordish activity or harassment could destroy your chances of a swift eviction.

How to reduce maintenance

Maintenance can be a killer for any landlord's profit margin and I have seen many a landlord suffer at the hands of 'the M word', as one of my landlords quite aptly called it. But I've seen a particular avoidable pattern happen over and over again.

Going back to the beginning of the book, when we looked at what types of properties to buy: potential future maintenance is something that you must really look at too. Old properties can cost you dearly and soon, with new eco regulations coming in, any properties that are not up to certain energy ratings will not be lettable, so be very aware of this in your future purchases.

Also be aware that modern properties that have been butchered by DIY enthusiasts can cost a fortune and be a complete can of worms. Thorough examinations and safety/building checks should be done to know exactly what you are taking on.

I once knew a property where the owner had sawn through the supporting struts attached to the joists in the roof space so that he could make headroom for a workshop. NOT GOOD.

But if you've already got your property, what can you do?

I've always found that the landlords who took on a property and embarked on a thorough refurbishment at the outset made much more profit in the long run, as they were not forever tormented by the M word. Get it all done at the outset; find out what is wrong or is going to go wrong at the beginning when the property is empty.

All the landlords I have ever known who have adopted the policy of 'just give it a coat of paint' suffer from bad tenants, void periods, compensating tenants for periods without heating, claims against them from tenants for damage to property or persons etc. It's just not worth it.

Letting property is a business, and due care and attention is required during the set-up to get it off to the right start. If you can't afford a refurbishment, then buy a newer or smaller property. It's just part of the outlay you need to accept with property.

One landlord, who had numerous ex-council properties and had never refurbished them properly, got to the situation where he just had no profit coming in at all, just through ongoing maintenance problems, even though he had bought the properties in the '90s at low prices and should have been making a fortune. We encouraged the landlord to embark on a programme of refurbishing every time one came empty, and he did. He now has a much healthier profit ledger, happier tenants who stay longer and a smile on his face.

So my advice here is to buy only what you can afford to do up properly, seek advice on works and get them done before you let a tenant near the place. Repairs can add up to being so much more expensive than a complete replacement in the end. They can also lead to tenants moving out due to being sick and tired of faults at the property, leading to a continual turnaround of tenants and excessive voids/letting fees.

Prevention is better than cure!

Maintenance and keeping tenants happy!

Tenants are generally quite simple creatures. They rented your house because they liked it, you and the location, and as long as they get what they expected they will generally keep quiet and send you the rent.

The most common cause of complaints from tenants nationwide in a recent survey was maintenance: properties being substandard, landlords not completing works on time, shoddy workmanship etc.

I've found that this is the biggest and most common reason why tenants move out of their properties; they have just had enough and are prepared to take their chances elsewhere.

When next thinking of the cost of a new boiler or fixing that overflow pipe that keeps dripping, remember the cost of a two-month void, re-letting fees etc. and all those evenings doing viewings. This might make you reconsider your plan and invest in getting the job done thoroughly.

Tenants at the end of the day are our customers and without them we have no business, but they are free agents and can go and rent whatever they want, wherever they want, quite easily and quickly.

As a landlord you have a legal obligation to keep your property in good repair at all times and if you fail to do so the tenant can report you to the council. Under the HHSRS the council can insist that you get the works done or, in extreme cases, they will do the work for you and bill you: not a pleasant scenario.

How to make property management easier and save your personal time

Property management can be one of the easiest jobs in the world if you're organised, or one of the hardest jobs in the world if you're not. It's your choice which one it's going to be for you. The secret to property management is mainly about having systems to ensure everything is monitored, a process to make sure required works are done and a checking procedure to pick up on any missed items or errors.

If your front end is set up right – if your paperwork and so on is all in order, as described in earlier sections – then the management at the back end will be infinitely easier. So really work on putting in place all the bits we have worked on so far.

If you have bought a property that suits your character, refurbished and furnished it properly to attract your target market, planned your marketing, referenced your tenants and ensured all your paperwork is correct, then you are nearly there.

Where so many landlords go wrong on the back end is in trying to do everything themselves. This can be a false economy. Time is one of the few resources we cannot buy back. Personally, I would prefer to spend a little money to get the right professional in to do a job correctly the first time, rather than tinker with it myself and upset the tenant further and end up paying later for someone to re-fix what I have done badly.

Identify what you are good at. If you are an organised office-type person, then maybe you should be running the back office system, but should you be fixing the tap?

Software

The back office system with a couple of properties can be completely manual, but if your goal is to get a lot of properties and eventually a larger portfolio, I would not hesitate to buy or lease a landlords' management software system. There are plenty on the market and they are all very similar.

You need to consider whether you want to buy a system and put it on your computer or lease a system, and there are definite advantages to both.

Buying a system means you pay once, download the product and then you are free to use it as you wish. There are no ongoing fees and the system will never change from what you have bought. The disadvantage of these systems is that as technology moves on, your system will not. There is no team of people 'tweaking' and improving it. There is also not generally a good back-end support structure as the system developers are not charging for that and therefore cannot provide it.

Leasing a system, you have a smaller up-front fee but will pay a monthly per-user fee. This will more than likely end up costing more overall, but you will have a team of system programmers continually updating the software on your behalf. This means that over time your software will evolve slightly and stay up to date. Leased systems normally offer a much stronger support network as they recognise that if they do not you will end the lease and go elsewhere. These systems are usually the best to go for if you are planning growth.

Security is important with software and data. Consider where the data is to be stored. Many of the leased systems are stored in server farms which are bullet-, bomb- and fireproof; this is a lot safer than your house in most cases.

Also you need to have a good system in place for backing up the software. If you have an in-house system, talk to a computer specialist and try to get automated backup software installed for security, or remember to make backups yourself regularly.

A word of warning: don't leave it too late! We tried for years to battle on with our own system that we had devised in-house, but because we are letting agents and not IT people, we had limited scope for development and we just could not keep up with technology. Eventually we found ourselves seriously left behind, so we had to make the huge leap to change to a new software package. By the time we changed systems we had over 18,000 records to transfer! It was a daunting task. It took us over two years to get the new system 100% as it should be, and cost me a lot of money in the process. What we did wrong was trying to do everything ourselves. We are not IT specialists and we should not have tried to be; we should have brought in the professionals sooner.

When deciding on a software package, look for ease of use. Can you move freely between the property record and the tenant record, the various landlord, tenant and contractor ledgers? Check that it will create yearly statements for your properties and ledger statements for your tenants.

A few features you would expect to see on your new software are as follows:

- **Arrears report.** This should tell you when your tenants fall into arrears and distinguish between different arrears levels: 7 days, 14 days, 21 days etc.

- **Gas and electric certificates due report.** This report should warn you a month before the gas certificates are due and allow you to send the work orders to the contractors all at the same time by clicking one button, rather than forcing you to deal with each certificate individually.

- **Renewals report.** This should tell you when your tenancies are expiring and when they are due for renewal. The software should be able to produce letters for your tenants en masse to ask them if they want to renew.

- **Inspection report.** There should be a report noting when your interim inspections are due and again producing letters en masse to tell the tenants when you will be going around.

- **Diary management.** Most systems will have an electronic diary; check if this can be seen over the internet so that you can check your diary from anywhere.

- **Outstanding actions.** The system should keep any actions that have not been completed, like maintenance, on an outstanding actions page for you to ensure they are followed up. This is usually on your diary.

- **Tenant matching.** When you have re-activated one of your properties or put a new property on, does the system allow you to search through all the tenants that have registered interest with you and send them text messages or emails to alert them of the new property available?

- **Tenant log-in.** Does your system allow your tenants to log in to see their ledgers and statements online?

Contractors

As a landlord you need a 'team' of professionals around you. Over the years we have used thousands of contractors and they range from downright useless to top experts in their field. Unfortunately until you start using them you have no idea what they are going to be like, as generally you can't judge them on face value. You need to have a process in place to monitor the contractors and trial new ones.

As a landlord you have a few legal responsibilities here too that you need to be aware of.

You must make sure that anyone whom you hire for a job in your house is 'qualified' to do the job. You have a duty to the contractor to ensure that he is safe himself, and you must also ensure that the tenant does not suffer harassment or problems as a result of any works the contractor carries out at the property.

So how can you ensure all these things? Firstly, before using any contractor you need to check that they have the experience, or in some cases the qualifications, to do what you want them to do.

With specialist tasks like gas or electric work, there are national registers you can check, where you should be able to find the contractor if you ask for their accreditation number or the name they are registered under. Remember, however, to ask for ID when the contractor attends so that you know they are the person they say they are. For gas you would look on the Gas Safe Register[6] and for electricians you could look on the ESC website,[7] as well as the individual accreditation sites.

---

[6] http://www.gassaferegister.co.uk/
[7] http://www.electricalsafetyfirst.org.uk/

Then for your own safety I would ask for copies of their public liability insurance to keep on file just in case they accidentally blow your house up. Following this, I would always trial any new contractors on small jobs first and then gradually increase the size of the job allocated. If this is not possible and you have to give them a big job like installing a new central heating system, then you inform them that as they are a new contractor, you will be getting another contractor to check their work when they have completed it. These aren't just words; you should actually get the second contractor in! For £30 or so it is money well spent and they will generally pick up something that has been missed.

Nowadays, you are expected to make sure that the contractor knows what to do if he comes across asbestos or has to go up a ladder, so you should also ask him for his health and safety policy stating how he would handle these situations if they arose, to satisfy yourself that you are happy with his proposed course of action.

This process has got me out of so many problems over the years. There was a big refurb on a client's property due and I was considering a contractor who went to my local BNI group and who claimed to be excellent at decorating and building work. Due to my process I asked them to do a smaller job first: a quick paint job on one of my flats that had become available recently (and which was about to be stripped and refurbished anyway), about two days' work. To my surprise they finished in only a few hours and I could not believe what I found!

They had left an inch-wide margin around the telephone connection box unpainted. They had not painted the wall behind the door, the skirting board was missed in so many places and in one spot it looked like they had painted around an object against the wall, as there was a hump of missed painting. The beam looked like they had wiped their brushes on it, not painted it, and to make the whole thing worse they had not used dust sheets; my whole carpet was splattered with paint! It was horrific, the worst job I have ever seen. Just imagine if that had been a client's job with building work as well! Lucky escape.

So the motto is 'do the paperwork, start them small, increase the size of the jobs as they do well and, when you feel ready to give them a bigger job, get one of your trusted contractors to check their work over'.

With regard to dealing with tenants, there are a few conversations that you need to have with contractors, as they can actually cause you more problems in the long run. Some contractors have a habit of 'scaring' tenants and can say things like, 'Ooh, you shouldn't be left with a shower like this; it could be lethal, you know.' This will give your tenants ammunition against you and in many cases it is just the contractor's opinion. You have asked them to go and solve any issues and report the faults to you, not scare the tenant to death.

For clarity, I'm not saying the contractor *shouldn't* tell the tenant if something is wrong; it's more about *how* they say what needs to be said. There are certain circumstances where a contractor has to inform the tenant of faults that can cause harm; for example, if a gas fire fails the check they must put a 'do not use' sticker on it and warn the tenant not to use it. Whatever the case, they must stick to the facts.

Accounts and deposits

As a landlord you have an obligation, if letting your property under assured shorthold tenancies, to register your tenants' deposits as soon as they move into the property and give you their money. You have two choices here: custodial or insurance-backed. Custodial means you forward your deposit to the provider and they will keep the deposit and at the end they will decide who has the deposit back. Insurance-backed refers to schemes where you are holding the deposit and the provider offers an arbitration service to determine where the deposit goes in the event of a dispute at the end of the tenancy.

If you opt for the insurance-backed scheme you must make sure that you put the money aside in a separate account. This is not your money; it is your tenant's money, which they have given to you to hold in trust until the end of the tenancy.

If you have not registered the deposit in one of the schemes then you will not be able to use a Section 21 notice to gain possession of your property and you could be liable to a fine of three times the deposit plus the deposit itself, to be payable to the tenant. So be careful to ensure that you select a deposit provider and follow the rules with regards to it.

Tenants' rents will normally be paid to you weekly or monthly by some form of standing order or BACS payment. You should be keeping a ledger of every payment that a tenant makes to you. If the tenant at any time asks you for a rent ledger you should issue this to them, and so you should have this information to hand.

A good software system will keep a ledger for you, but in the absence of such, then an Excel spreadsheet or rent book could be used instead. If your tenant pays their rent weekly then they will need to be issued a rent book.

The Deposit Protection Service[8] and Tenancy Deposit Scheme[9] websites may be useful here.

To summarise

Overall the key to happy management is to buy the right property in the first place and do a thorough refurbishment on it to prevent works later. Check that you have selected the right mode of marketing your property for your target market and get those photos and descriptions up to scratch as well as the property presentation.

Invest in good paperwork and keep it up to date; ensure everything is produced and signed as it should be and filed away safely.

Have a referencing procedure and be strict on its criteria, to reduce your chances of any bad tenants getting into one of your properties initially.

Jump on any arrears immediately, but professionally and non-emotionally to avoid any potential harassment claims

Deal with any maintenance immediately. Leaving maintenance too long can cost you dearly in the form of tenant loss and re-letting fees or, even worse, an order through the council.

---

[8]   http://www.depositprotection.com
[9]   http://www.thedisputeservice.co.uk

Invest in good management software and learn how to use it to its full capacity.

Manage your contractors and build up a reliable team around you that will safely look after you, your tenants and your property.

The Law!

Tenancy law

Law of the land versus contract law

Whatever country we are in has laws which, purely by being in the country, we agree to abide by. These are laws of the land. In many cases we are not aware of most of them, but they are there waiting to catch us out if we break one of them.

Most of us are aware of the ones below:

- Don't kill.

- Don't steal.

- Drive on the left.

- Don't sell alcohol unless licensed.

There are literally tens of thousands of laws out there, though, and we cannot possibly know all of them. You are probably not aware of some of these!

- It is an act of treason to place a postage stamp bearing the British monarch upside down.

- It is illegal for a cab in the City of London to carry rabid dogs or corpses.

- It is illegal to die in the Houses of Parliament.

- In Lancashire, no person is permitted, after being asked to stop by a constable, to incite a dog to bark on the seashore.

- In the UK, a pregnant woman can legally relieve herself anywhere she wants – even, if she so requests, in a policeman's helmet.

- In Chester, Welshmen are banned from entering the city before sunrise and from staying after sunset.
  With thanks to: Donald Stewart at Faegre & Benson, John Barnett at Burges Salmon, Robert Crossley at Walker Morris, James Odds at Matthew Arnold & Baldwin, and Dan Kieran, author of I Fought the Law *(Bantam Press). And the* Times.

When you go into any type of business you will become aware of many more laws that start to apply to you with regard to employment, taxation, VAT, trade, import, export and contracts. A couple are:

- Contracts have to be fair.

- Contracts must consist of 'an offer, an acceptance and a consideration'.

In business, you will produce contracts with your clients. These are regulated by 'contract law'. If you produce contracts of trade for people to sign and to be committed to, then you have a duty to ensure that the contracts you have asked them to sign are fair and do not overburden the individual. If they were to contest the contract by saying that the contract is 'unfair', a court could render the contract or a particular clause null and void and therefore useless.

In order for a contract to be valid there are a few things also that need to be considered. The contract needs to contain an 'offer', an 'acceptance' and a 'consideration'.

An example of this would be if I agree to rent you my car ('the offer'). You agree to hire it for six weeks ('the acceptance'), for which you will give me £660 ('the consideration'). This would be a valid contract in the eyes of the law.

A few example of agreements covered by contract law are:

- Car hire agreements

- Lease agreements

- Goods and supply contracts

This contract will all be valid as long as they contain an offer, an acceptance and a consideration ... or will they?

Example

I, Sally Lawson, give you, ..., the right to drive on the right-hand side of the road throughout the UK and you agree to do so. For this you agree to pay me £20.

I, ..., accept your offer.

Signed ....

Signed ....

Dated ....

So here we have a valid contract, with an offer (to drive on the right), an acceptance (you agree to do so) and a consideration (£20). We could both sign it and agree it and it would be a valid contract in the eyes of contract law, wouldn't it?

No, of course it wouldn't. Why not? Because the contract is giving permission for something that violates the law of the land and therefore would not be valid. I also do not have the authority to grant such an offer.

So what can we learn from this with regard to being a landlord? As landlords, when drawing up contracts, we have to abide by contract law (making sure that the contracts are fair and that there is an offer, an acceptance and a consideration), but we also have to abide by the myriad of housing and tenancy laws that exist (laws of the land). You cannot overrule the laws of the land; you must abide by them. Even if you do not refer to them, they are there regardless and could render your contract null and void.

So with this in mind you need to be really careful in drawing up your contracts. You should be fully aware of all the laws and regulations that apply to you in order to make sure you are not falling foul of these.

Some key legislation relating to housing law that you need to be aware of:

- Law of Property Act 1925

- Health and Safety at Work Act 1974

- Protection from Eviction Act 1977

- Housing Act 1985

- Housing Act 1988 and revisions in 1996

- Consumer Protection Act 1987

- Furniture and Furnishings (Fire) (Safety) Regulations 1988

- Gas Safety (Installation and Use) Regulations 1994, 1996 and 1998

- Finance Act 1995

- Electrical Equipment Regulations 1994

- Housing Act 2004

The history of the assured shorthold tenancy agreement

A great way to understand the laws is to understand the process by which those laws came about: to understand where we have come from and how we got to here. In other words, to understand the history of the assured shorthold tenancy or AST, which is the most commonly used tenancy agreement today.

The early twentieth century

Try to imagine what life was like for a typical tenant in 1900. Think of Scrooge and *Oliver Twist*. Landlords were wealthy land owners or factory owners.

There was a huge gap between the wealth of the landlords and the poor. Accommodation in many cases was provided by the wealthy for their employees and often would have been linked to the continuous employment of the tenant, meaning if they ceased employment they would lose the house.

Tenants would have had virtually no rights. If the landlord wanted them out, he could merely change the locks and remove their stuff at will, and many did. The employer or landlord had complete control.

At this time most people lived in privately rented accommodation and the percentage of properties privately rented was a shocking 90%.

Mortgages were not available to the poor, and gathering the deposits would have been impossible anyway. The rich were rich and the poor were poor and that was just the way it was.

The country went through two world wars, which resulted in many homes being destroyed. This led to a shortage of accommodation, and councils started to build council accommodation to meet the new demand.

1954 and 1977

The Landlord and Tenant Act 1954 tightened up the laws regarding tenancy agreements, which were further tightened by the Protection from Eviction Act 1977. These gave new 'security of tenure' rights to tenants by the creation of 'protected and statutory tenancies', which gave tenants the right to remain in the property for life and also two rights of succession to relatives.

For landlords this was a huge problem. If you rented your house out to a tenant now, you might not get it back in your lifetime. Suddenly landlords were not in the driving seat and many backed away from providing private rented accommodation.

1987

By 1987 the PRS (Private Rented Sector) had plummeted from 90% at the turn of the century to 7% of all housing stock being privately rented.

This was a huge problem. The councils were not building council accommodation any more, the country was gripped in a recession, mines were closing and the country was experiencing its highest ever unemployment figures.

The government at the time researched the world economies and found that when a country had a higher percentage of its populace in private rented accommodation, it also had very low unemployment rates.

In France and Germany, for example, the private rented sectors were 33% and 41% respectively. These countries were experiencing low levels of unemployment because the population were mobile, able to move to where the work was.

Our government, however, were struggling with recession, high unemployment, the miners' strikes etc. and an un-mobile workforce, stuck in properties they owned or on long-term tenancies. The government felt that if you were a tenant on a short-term lease and you lost your job, you would be able to move to where the work was: something you would be unable or unlikely to do if you were trapped by a mortgage. This was a story that was being played out in industrial towns across the country at that time as manufacturing plants closed down all over the United Kingdom.

The Housing Act 1988

So the government spent 250 hours in parliament revising the housing sector and in 1988 launched the **Housing Act 1988**.

The Housing Act 1988 completely revised the rights of landlords and tenants, giving the private rented sector a new lease of life. Landlords could again get their properties back at the end of a tenancy and had grounds established on which they could gain possession of their property if they needed to.

This did the trick and again landlords started investing in rented accommodation, filling the need that was growing from an ever-expanding population and creating a more flexible workforce. Demand for rented accommodation was also increasing due to immigration, divorce, moving employment and people now wanting to live alone.

On the **15th January 1989**, the Housing Act 1988 came into effect. All tenancies would now automatically be 'assured tenancies' as long as the tenant's circumstances met certain criteria:

- They must be an individual.

- The property must be their main or principal residence.

- They must have 'exclusive possession' of at least part of the property.

- The landlord must not be resident.

If the tenant meets all these criteria then they are entitled to an 'assured shorthold tenancy' or 'assured tenancy' agreement. If they do not meet the criteria above then their tenancy agreement would be 'outside the act', which means that the terms of the Housing Act 1988 would not apply to them and you would need to refer to the Protection from Eviction Act 1977 and contract law.

The original 1988 act stated that, in order to create an assured shorthold tenancy, landlords had to serve a Section 20 notice. If they failed to serve this before the commencement of the tenancy then what they in fact had created was an assured tenancy. The act also stated that, if a landlord wanted to seek possession of his property from a tenant for nonpayment of rent, he could do so when the tenant was three months in arrears.

This, it was decided, needed to be improved further. The housing act was revised in 1996 and the revisions took effect on the **28th February 1997**.

These changes meant that any tenancies created from this point were automatically assured shorthold tenancies, not assured tenancies, and this meant that the Section 20 notice was no longer required to create an assured shorthold tenancy. The arrears required before the landlord could seek possession were also reduced from three months to two, which was a welcome change in the landlord's favour.

The Housing Act 2004

In 2004 the government brought out the **Housing Act 2004**, creating the HHSRS (Housing Health and Safety Rating System), a blueprint for acceptable standards in rented accommodation with regards to safety and condition, and giving powers to local councils to take action on negligent landlords swiftly.

It also tightened up the definition for the 'house in multiple occupation' or HMO, which leads to the rules we have now for situations in which three or more non-related people share a rented property, and it introduced licensing as mandatory for HMO properties where there are five or more residents over three floors.

The Housing Act 2004 also made provisions with regard to the registration of deposits, leading to the deposit regulations that we now have.

The present day and the future

Now, in 2015, the private rented sector stands at 18% and is set to grow to a predicted 20% by 2019, and it has been mentioned that it could achieve 50% by 2050! So the PRS is going to become an absolutely integral part of our society's make-up.

Which contracts should you use?

Well, now you understand that the laws of the land prevail in all circumstances, which means there is no point in trying to take away a tenant's rights by putting something different in a contract as their rights still remain. One of the most common landlord errors I have seen is that they issue an AST and tell the tenant that they can give the tenant one month's notice to vacate. This is not the case; the tenant has an automatic right to two months' notice, no matter what the contract says, because a tenancy agreement cannot overrule laws of the land or housing law.

So it is important to spend a little time to understand who your tenant is actually going to be and under which contract they should be set. If they are not eligible for an assured or assured shorthold tenancy, then they will be entitled to a common law or contractual tenancy agreement instead. These contracts are more flexible on the landlord's part, but reference is needed to the Protection from Eviction Act 1977 and the laws of fair contracts.

Some examples of agreements that are outside the Housing Act 1988

The general name for all of these types of agreements is 'common law' or 'contractual' tenancy agreements, but they have also been given more specific names, which you might be familiar with. These are all agreements that are not governed by the rules of the Housing Act 1988.

- **Holiday lets:** when letting a property for holiday purposes.

- **Educational bodies**: this is for educational bodies themselves, rather than private landlords, letting to students.

- **Agricultural lets:** where there are more than two acres of land.

- **Company lets:** where a property is being let to a company, usually for the use of their directors or employees.

- **High/low rent:** below £250pcm or above £1,000pcm.

- **Pre-1989 lets:** any contract entered into before 15th January 1989 will be outside the protection of the Housing Act 1988.

- **Resident landlord:** if the landlord is resident then his tenants are not entitled to an assured shorthold tenancy and he will generally offer them a licence agreement.

- **Commercial lets:** where the letting is for commercial use as opposed to residential.

Housing Act 1988 tenancy

In order for the tenant to qualify for an assured shorthold tenancy, the following criteria must be met:

- The tenant must be an individual.

- The tenant must have exclusive possession of all or part of the dwelling.

- The dwelling must be the tenant's main or principal residence.

- The landlord must not be resident.

On the next page is a flowchart that you can use to identify what type of tenancy agreement you should be using.

Flowchart of which tenancy agreement to use

Tenancy Agreement Checker
Are You Aware You May Have Used The Wrong Tenancy Agreement?

YES Individual with accommodation not linked to employment

Principal residence — **NO** — Exclusive possession of at least one room? — **NO**

NO — Exclusive possession of at least one room? — **NO** — Licence

YES — Non-Housing Act tenancy agreement — **YES** — Licence

YES — NHA tenancy agreement protected by 'protection from eviction act' 1977

YES

Landlord resident? — **YES** — Licence

Why not double check right now?

NO

Exclusive possession of at least one room? — **NO** — Licence

Simply follow this flow diagram to quickly and easily ensure you have the right agreement in place and rest assured that you are legally covered... or perhaps you may need to make some changes to the agreement you currently use to ensure all your future tenancies are compliant and solid.

YES — Assured Shorthold Tenancy

You can't believe everything you read!

With all the talk of creating fair contracts, easy-to-read agreements etc you would expect that a reasonably drafted agreement could be understood by anyone. But this is not always the case. There are a few things to keep an eye out for.

Below is an example of a clause; similar ones to this are in all tenancy agreements across the country and have to be in order to allow the landlord to terminate his contract, but it is far from clear.

The forfeiture clause:

> *The landlord has the right to automatically repossess the property (subject to his statutory rights to do so) in the event of the tenant becoming 14 days in arrears, whether legally demanded or not.*

Many landlords, upon reading this clause in their contract, believe that they have the right to change the locks after the rent being due for more than 14 days, but can they?

No, they can't, but why not?

Well, you already know that statutory laws say that you have to wait for the tenant to be two months in arrears. Does that mean that the clause is misleading?

What most people fail to register is the bit in the brackets: *subject to his statutory rights to do so.* They don't understand it, so they ignore it. But obviously the landlord does not have any statutory rights to repossess the property after 14 days and therefore he cannot do that, even if the clause seems to suggest he can.

It's a valid clause and it needs to be in the agreements, but it's a great demonstration of how to a layperson a legal agreement can be very misleading indeed, if taken at face value.

To summarise

Legal contracts are best drawn up by a legal expert in the relevant type of tenancy. If you attempt to use your own contract, then make sure you are well read in the laws that relate to you and understand the implications and references of the clauses stated within the contract.

Giving notice on your tenant when you want to get your tenant out

There are two types of notice to serve on your tenant if you want them to leave under an assured shorthold tenancy agreement: the Section 8 notice and the Section 21 notice.

These two notices serve different purposes and are to be used in different situations. The Section 8 notice is used when you want to cite one of the 17 grounds prescribed for use by a landlord to regain possession of a property, under the Housing Act 1988 & 1996. The other is used when you just want to get your property back at the end of the tenancy.

The Section 8 notice

The Section 8 notice is basically a notice that says that you as the landlord are seeking possession of the property under one of the prescribed grounds for possession. You will need to be fully aware of the ground or grounds you want to use, along with the full wording of that ground, before you issue the Section 8 notice.

All the grounds are numbered in the Housing Act and they fall into three different classifications. All of them allow you to seek possession from a tenant; however, some of them will only apply in certain circumstances and there are different 'notice periods' for all of them.

Which is the best ground to use?

There are various grounds you can use to gain possession. Whichever ground you use you must word in full on the Section 8 notice, in order for the notice to be valid. The wordings used below are not the full wordings.

Grounds are broken down into three types:

- Prior notice: 1–5 (notice has to be served before commencement of tenancy)

- Mandatory: 1–8 (judge has to award possession if ground is proven)

- Discretionary: 9–17 (judge may use his discretion in deciding whether to grant possession)

Prior notice (1–5)

To use a prior notice ground, a landlord has to serve a notice on the tenant stating that he may wish to use a prior notice ground at some point during the tenancy to seek possession. If this notice is not served before the tenancy begins, the landlord will not be able to use these grounds later on.

Common prior notice grounds used in cases where the landlord is renting out his former own home are the 'mortgagee clause' (ground 2) and the 'landlord's main home clause' (ground 1). Both allow notice to be served to gain possession if so required. Many mortgage companies will insist on these grounds being included with a residential mortgage (not a buy-to-let).

Below is the full list of mandatory prior notice grounds; however the following are summaries, not the actual full wordings that you will need to use on the notice.

1. Landlord used to live in the property.

2. The mortgagee is claiming possession.

3. The property was let for a holiday at some point in the year before the tenancy started.

4. The property was let by an educational body at some point in the year before the tenancy started.

5. The property is held for use by a minister of religion.

Mandatory grounds (1–8)

These are the grounds on which the court MUST award you possession, as long as your paperwork is in order, if you can prove in court that the circumstances are as stated in one of these grounds.

The most common 'mandatory' ground is the rent arrears ground or Ground 8, which can be used when one of the following applies (on a tenancy that began after the 15th January 1989):

- On a weekly tenancy: the tenant is eight weeks in arrears.

- On a monthly tenancy: the tenant is two months in arrears.

- On a quarterly tenancy: the tenant is three months in arrears.

If you can prove with your ledger statement that the tenant was this amount in arrears at the time of serving the notice and at the time of appearing at court, then the judge, subject to all other paperwork being correct, must award in your favour for possession.

Below is the full list of mandatory grounds; however the following are summaries, not the actual full wordings. Bear in mind that grounds 1–5 are also prior notice grounds.

1. Landlord used to live in the property.

2. The mortgagee is claiming possession.

3. The property was let for a holiday at some point in the year before the tenancy started.

4. The property was let by an educational body at some point in the year before the tenancy started.

5. The property is held for use by a minister of religion.

6. The landlords wish to re-develop the property.

7. The tenant has died (unless someone has a right to succeed).

8. The tenant owed two months' rent (assuming monthly tenancy) both at the time of serving the notice and at the time of appearing at court.

Discretionary grounds (9–17)

These are the 'possible' grounds. You may get possession but it is not guaranteed. Grounds 10 and 11, 'an amount of rent in arrears' and 'persistently in arrears', are the most commonly relied upon of these; these are usually served alongside Ground 8 ('more than two months in arrears') in case the tenant decides to pay a little rent just before court day, to keep their arrears just below the two months and prevent you from being awarded possession under Ground 8.

There are many other grounds available to use. In practice, due to the expense of attending court and the potential upset it can cause, most landlords would not attempt court on a discretionary ground alone, unless they had lots of evidence to back themselves up and the situation was really intolerable. But discretionary grounds can be tagged onto the Section 8 notice alongside a mandatory ground to add a little more weight.

Below is the full list of discretionary grounds; however, the following are summaries, not the actual full wordings.

9. Suitable alternative accommodation is available.

10. The tenant was behind with their rent at the point of serving the notice and when the landlord started court proceedings.

11. The tenant has been persistently behind with their rent.

12. The tenant has broken one or more of their obligations under their tenancy agreement.

13. The condition of the premises or the common parts of the property has deteriorated due to the actions of the tenant.

14. The tenant, or someone visiting the tenant, is guilty of causing a nuisance or annoying the neighbours. Alternatively, the tenant has been convicted of using the property for illegal or immoral purposes (or of allowing someone else to use the property for such purposes), or has been convicted of an arrestable offence.

15. The condition of the furniture has deteriorated due to the actions of the tenant.

16. The property was granted for the tenant to carry out their duties and the tenant is no longer employed by the landlord.

17. The landlord was induced to grant a tenancy by false statements given by the tenant.

How to serve

Different grounds have different notice periods that you have to wait for, once you have served the Section 8 citing the relevant grounds, before you can commence court action. For example, with grounds 8, 10 and 11, you have to give the tenant 14 days' notice that you are going to take the matter to court. With Ground 14 there is no notice period – you can start court action immediately – and with Ground 1, the notice period is two months. Just make sure you have the correct notice period before you serve the Section 8 notice.

You can serve the Section 8 notice on your tenant by hand or by post. You need to allow an additional two working days for service when serving by post.

Once you have served the notice, go to the www.courtservice. gov.uk website, download the 'certificate of service' form,[1] complete it and keep it in your file for later use. This is just a notice stating that you have served the Section 8 Notice and how and when you did it.

The Section 21 notice

The Section 21 notice is the notice you use when you just want your property back. The tenant does not have to have defaulted in any way for this to be used. You will, however, have to be at

---

[1]   The list of forms can be found at this location: http://www.justice .gov.uk/courts/procedure-rules/civil/forms

the end of your contract, and it cannot be used before six months have passed. For example, if you have a tenant move in on a three-month assured shorthold tenancy and they fail to move out, you will not be able to issue a Section 21 notice to expire before the end of the six-month period, even though your contract has expired.

A Section 21 has to give two full months' notice to a tenant, so make sure that you are really careful with your issuing dates. Allow two days for service if delivering it by post, one if by hand. More than two months' notice can be given if you wish, but the minimum is two months.

If a contract is coming to an end, use a 21(1)b notice; if it has expired, then use the 21(4)a notice.

Example

> *Hi, Mr Tenant. Here's your six-month tenancy agreement, if you would like to sign this and your inventory and statement. We're also serving this Section 21 notice; it's just to say that we MAY wish to have the property back at the end of the tenancy agreement, but if you and we are happy to renew you will be sent a renewal contract!*

Five months later:

> *Subject to the notice given at outset of tenancy we require possession in one month.*

NOT FAIR OR CORRECT!

Above is an example of common practice for many years amongst landlords, and this is to serve the Section 21 at the beginning of the tenancy, immediately after the signing of the tenancy agreement.

If you will absolutely definitely want the property back at the end of six months and tell the tenants that, then that is fine. If you are just issuing the notice early to try to get out of having to give them two clear months' notice later, however, this is completely wrong and defrauding the tenant out of their right to two months' notice.

Court actions and the court paperwork

So you have issued your Section 21 or your Section 8 or maybe even both! The end date has come and gone; now it's time to proceed to the next step of taking the tenant to court.

Many landlords fear going to court to pursue an eviction, but it's generally not as scary as you think, so let's dispel the myths.

The courtroom is just a room with a judge who will sit at the head of the table with you on one side and your tenant the other side. There is no jury and no witnesses.

You will have your opportunity to explain what the problem is and why you are there, and present your paperwork and ledgers or anything else the judge wants to see from the file. The tenant will then say why they think possession should not be granted.

The judge (subject to being happy with all you have said and your paperwork matching) will ask you what you want. You will normally ask for a 14-day possession order, arrears and court fee. The judge may grant this or may give the tenant up to six weeks to leave and will then let you know of the decision.

You thank the judge and leave. It generally takes no more than a few minutes in most cases.

You cannot start court action until you have served your Section 8 or 21 and the time for this has expired. When the notice period is finished the next step is to visit www.courtservice.gov.uk and download the forms you need to start proceedings.

For a possession with rent arrears you will need to follow the standard eviction procedure and prepare the following paperwork:

- Particulars of claim.

- Certificate of service (to prove service, from the court service website).

- Ledger statement (from your system, showing all the rental payments made and due).

- Copy of AST signed by tenant.

- Copy of notice served (Section 21 or 8 or both).

- N5 claim form for possession of property (court service website).

- Court fee.

Once you have all of the above documentation ready and completed (there are guidance notes on the court service website to help you with completion if you need help), you need to make a copy for each of the tenants (and guarantors if applicable) and a copy for the courts and then go to the court office to lodge the claim.

The first few times you do this, it's a good idea to visit the court office and ask them to check through the papers for you there and then, just in case you have made any mistakes, as this will save valuable time.

Many courts now allow you to log claims online, too.

The court process

Once you have lodged your claim papers, it is a bit of a waiting game, but you must keep an eye on the time as if you do not hear anything for a couple of weeks it's a good idea to chase things up. I have had courts lose papers before now, so keep on top of them and call if you are concerned.

Eventually you will get a date for the hearing; this will usually be in about four to six weeks, depending on how busy the court is. Put this in your diary.

Before you attend, work out your daily rental amount, and ensure you have all of your paperwork with you and in an order that you understand. On the day of the court hearing, arrive in plenty of time, let the court official know you are there and wait to be called.

When you are called, follow the court official to the hearing room and make yourself comfortable, making sure you have all your papers in front of you. You need to appear calm, organised, knowledgeable and ready.

Answer any questions asked of you and be ready to tell the judge what you want: possession, rent arrears and court fee.

At the end say, 'Thank you,' and walk away calmly. Never be aggressive or humiliate the judge, even if they are wrong. You can correct the judge, but be polite and courteous at all times; you do not want to make an enemy of him. You may be seeing him again!

You will receive a notification of the judgement in the post shortly after the hearing and then wait.

Bailiffs

On the day after the tenant is supposed to be out, go and visit the property and check if they have left. If there are any signs of them still being there, walk away and apply for a 'warrant of execution' with the bailiff's office, which is also in the court.

Go to the bailiff's office, complete the warrant form and pay the fee required, and they will give you a date; this is usually around two to six weeks away. On the date that you are given, attend the property with the bailiff and someone to change the locks. If you suspect that the tenant is not going to leave (99% of them will have gone by this date) then you will need to call police assistance. If you think they have left a dog behind, you may also need to arrange a dog handler to attend to remove the dog.

Safety regulations

Gas Safety (Installation and Use) Regulations 1996/1998

- Check gas every year.

Many of you will know that you have to renew the gas certificate every year for a rental property. The penalties for not doing this are a maximum of six months in jail and / or a £5,000 fine for each offence.

- Schedule gas checks.

You need to ensure that you keep some sort of diarised system to make sure that you are not left with expired gas certificates, as this is your responsibility. Some contractors will offer to do this for you, but you still need to keep on top of this yourself as you are the one prosecuted if it is not done. The same applies if you are letting through a letting agent.

- Keep records for two years.

Both you and the contractor (and the agent if you are using one) have a responsibility to keep records for two years of any gas works carried out at the property and any gas certificates. Make sure you keep these safe and can put your hand to them quickly if need be. Always remember to read the certificates when you get them back in from the contractors, too, as although they may say 'pass' there may be urgent works required to be done within a 28-day timescale. Failing to follow these up will invalidate the certificate.

- Give gas certificate to tenant before they move in.

Every tenant has to receive a copy of the gas certificate BEFORE moving in to the property, and it needs to say 'pass' or 'safe'.

- Give renewals to each tenant within 28 days.

When you carry out renewal gas certificates, each year or on a material change, you need to remember to send a copy to your tenants within 28 days of it being done. In the case of an HMO the certificate needs to be displayed in a prominent position.

- Leases over seven years are excluded.

If your lease to your tenant is for more than seven years (meaning that the initial term is more than seven years, and the tenant cannot end it before seven years, as there is no break clause), then the property will fall outside these regulations and gas certificate renewals are not your responsibility. However, you should still make sure that your property is safe, as you will be liable under other regulations.

- Tenants' appliances *may be* excluded.

If a tenant tells you that they are going to fit their own gas appliance, you need to be careful. Always make sure that it says in your tenancy agreement that the tenant has to get your consent before fitting any gas appliances. You need to be sure of the intentions of the tenant before agreeing to their doing so. If the tenant is planning on taking the item with them when they leave (get this in writing), then it is their responsibility to maintain the gas appliance and get it checked; however, if they intend to leave the appliance then it will become the landlord's responsibility to maintain it and have it checked, so get a new gas certificate for it.

Be careful here: if a tenant wants to install a gas appliance to the landlord's flue, the landlord may be responsible for costly flue work. (This could also be called a 'relevant flue'; the term 'relevant' in the regulations refers to items that are the landlord's responsibility.)

- Do not 'contract out'.

When the regulations first came out, many landlords tried to put in their contracts that it was the tenant's responsibility to get the gas certificates done, but this is not acceptable and cannot be done; it is always the responsibility of the landlord. Even if the landlord passes this responsibility to an agent, the landlord is still liable under these regulations, although the landlord may also have a separate claim against an agent if the agent fails to perform his duties in this regard.

- Room-sealed appliances in bathroom and bedrooms.

Any appliance fitted in a bathroom or bedroom must be 'room-sealed'. Be wary of loft bedroom conversions and open-plan set-ups here. An appliance may 'technically' be in the lounge, but if this is linked via an open-plan layout to the bedroom, it still needs to be checked by an engineer for safety.

- Gas fires in bedrooms to be under 14kW.

Any fire placed in a bedroom or sleeping area must be under 14kW, for safety.

- Beware of changes of use!

Be wary of tenants using lounges to sleep in or changing the use of rooms to sleeping areas, as you could quite easily fall foul of the regulations here. This is why it is important to check your properties regularly for any changes.

- £5,000 fine, six months in jail!

These are the maximum penalties under this regulation and they can be applied for each offence, so in the case of an HMO you could have six or more claims against you from each tenant. In a serious case, you may also be liable for further penalties under other safety regulations that may apply.

Questions

Whoops! What should you do?

- You do everything you should do and carry out your gas safety check. After this, though, you turn the through lounge into two rooms and fit double glazing!

- You do an inspection and you notice that the tenants are using the lounge as a bedroom right next to the open-fronted living flame gas fire!

Which law would you break?

You have to renew the gas certificate, and if you don't you run the risk of six months in jail or a £5,000 fine!

However, the tenant won't let you in, so you can't enter! (Due to harassment laws the penalties for infringing on a tenant's right to quiet enjoyment can be severe!)

Which law would you break? **Answer at the back.**

Electrical Equipment Regulations 1994

These regulations relate to the supply of electrical equipment that has been designed with a working voltage of between 50 and 1,000 volts AC (or between 75 and 1,500 DC). They act as a secondary legislation under the Consumer Protection Act 1987 ('the Act'). Because these regulations have the same definition of 'supplier' as the Consumer Protection Act, landlords letting in the course of business are liable as suppliers.

The regulations make it the obligation of the supplier to ensure that the equipment is 'safe'. This is described in Section 19 of the Act: a 'safe' item poses no risk of death or injury to humans or pets, or of property damage.

- Section 19 and Section 39.

Section 19 of the Consumer Protection Act 1987 states that a 'supplier' must ensure that their property is safe so as not to cause injury, death or damage to humans, animals or property.

Section 39 of the Consumer Protection Act 1987 states that it is a defence to show in court that you have taken 'all reasonable steps' to avoid committing an offence. So the questions you need to ask yourself before letting out a property to a tenant are:

Have you done everything you could have done to avoid committing an offence?

Are you sure that the property is safe?

How would you prove that it was safe in a court of law?

Without a third-party electrical certificate, it would certainly be difficult to prove your property's safety.

Some tenants make a profession out of taking legal action against unaware landlords. Imagine the scenario. You move a tenant into a property and you are sure everything is safe, but you do not do an electrical inspection because you do not feel it necessary. The next thing you hear is the tenant complaining that her two-year-old son has just nearly died by sticking his finger around the badly-fitted sleeve of a plug attached to the fridge.

You are baffled because you were sure that the plug was a factory-fitted moulded plug, but you have no evidence. The tenant, however, does have evidence of a loose, badly-fitted, incorrectly-fused plug and goes to the health and safety executive. What would be your defence? What would be your proof?

This is why it is so important to have electrical inspections done before you allow a tenant to move into the property, to protect yourself as well as the tenant, to give you proof of the property's compliance and to show in court that you have done all that you could have done.

- Supply instruction booklets.

Under the electrical equipment regulations, the tenant must be provided with an operation manual or booklet for any electrical appliance in the property. This means that you should have the instruction booklets in a folder somewhere, and mentioned on the inventory, for every single electrical appliance (lamp, fridge etc.) in the house. Often these booklets can be downloaded off the internet. Remember to keep a copy, though, in case they get lost by a tenant, as it might be difficult to get a replacement.

- Buy new electrical items or have second-hand ones checked.

As a landlord it is generally best practice to only buy new electrical appliances for your rented property. If you do supply second-hand or used electrical appliances to a tenant, you will need to get an electrical certificate done on the property to prove its safety and compliance and keep this certificate on record.

If an appliance is new then there is no need to have it checked for the first year, as long as you keep the receipt.

- Check plugs and sockets to ensure they are fitted and fused correctly.

There is a regulation dedicated solely to plugs and sockets, but in brief: you have a responsibility to ensure that your electrical appliances are all fitted with a moulded or securely fitted plug, with insulated pins and the correct fuse for the appliance it is attached to.

To summarise

The electrical regulations come under the Consumer Protection Act 1987, so sections 19 and 39 of the Act apply to the electrical regulations too.

In order to be able to show as a defence in court that you took all reasonable steps to avoid committing an offence, it is advisable to have the electrics checked by a competent and suitably qualified engineer to ensure compliance.

Ensure you supply instruction booklets for all electrical appliances provided at your rented property.

Buy only new electrical items or have second-hand ones checked by a competent and qualified electrician to ensure and prove they are safe.

Check plugs and sockets to ensure they are fitted and fused correctly, then either carry a certificate to show these were checked or state on your inventory that these have been checked.

Consumer Protection Act 1987

- Relates to ALL of property and the contents supplied by a landlord.

- Section 19 of 'the Act': the property and its contents must be safe so as not to cause injury, death or damage to humans, pets or property.

- Section 39 of 'the Act': it is a defence to show that you have taken all reasonable steps to avoid committing the offence.

Furniture and Furnishings (Fire) (Safety) Regulations 1988

These regulations stipulate that the 'supplier' of any soft furnishings, i.e. the landlord, must ensure that they are 'safe' for use and meet the current fire safety and match-resistance tests.

Simply checking that the furniture carries a label stating that it is compliant will tell you that the furniture meets with the regulations, but you also need to protect yourself so that you can prove in court that it *was* compliant if need be. For example, a mattress could be swapped for a non-compliant one and you could struggle to show that the mattress shown to the health and safety executive by the tenant is not the one you supplied without some sort of proof. Ensure you keep records and know where they are.

According to the 1988 regulations, furniture sold after 1st March 1990 must comply with the current regulations for fire and safety and must carry labels (sewn into the hems) to prove compliance. Beware, though: there is a 'black market' for safety labels, and I have come across many 'sewn-in' labels. They are, however, easy to spot as the original label should actually be sewn into a hem of the furniture to prevent fraud; this is not easy to do post-manufacture, so the fake ones tend to look very badly sewn.

If you do not have these labels on the furniture that you want to supply, you will need to get the furniture checked to show that it is compliant. This can be expensive and difficult to prove, so make sure that your tenants and workmen are aware that they should not remove any labels that are fitted.

If the label has been lost but the item does conform to regulations, a receipt is proof. Any items pre-1950s are OK as they did not use the flammable filling before this decade; however, the problem is demonstrating when the item was manufactured.

Any items that do not have labels and are not compliant will need to be removed and replaced with new furniture to be safe.

Avoid second-hand furniture; however, if you must buy second-hand, ensure that anything you buy carries the relevant labels to show compliance. Be wary of buying furniture off vacating tenants.

It is an offence to give, sell or in any way pass a non-compliant item of furniture to the tenants, so do not be tempted to leave it in the garage, advertise it as free to collect etc. as this is against the regulations

The penalties for non-compliance are a £5,000 fine and/or six months' imprisonment, so this is a very serious offence.

The regulations here do not apply to carpets and curtains.

To summarise

Only buy new furniture and keep the receipts.

Remove all old furniture or any furnishings that do not carry labels.

Keep a record of all furniture and its labels or get it checked by a suitably qualified third party.

Do not pass non-compliant furniture to a tenant under any circumstances.

Going overseas? Know about the non-resident landlord tax or NRL

The law states under the Finance Act 1995 that the last person to have the landlord's rent before it gets into the landlord's bank account is responsible for paying tax on the landlord's behalf; this is to ensure that the government collects its tax. However, if you are going overseas and renting out a property in the UK you can get around this.

Before you leave you need to complete an NRL exemption request form. This is a request to Revenue and Customs to trust you to pay your tax. It will give your letting agent (or the last person touching your rent before it goes to you) an exemption number. This means that the collector of the rent can forward the rent to you free of deductions. You will then do your tax return at the end of the year in the normal manner.

You need to remember that the exemption number here remains the property of the collector of the rent and therefore if you change agents, you will need to complete a new NRL exemption request form.

To summarise

If you are going overseas, then as a landlord you need to complete the NRL exemption form available at www.hmrc. gov.uk and submit it to Revenue and Customs with details of who will be your UK agent or the last collector of your monies.

Houses in multiple occupation: know the rules!

- Three or more non-related individuals in a property: HMO

- Seven or more residents: planning required to convert to an HMO

- Five residents or more over three storeys or more: licensable HMO

What is an HMO?

The Housing Act 2004 made very clear and far-reaching amendments as to what was to be classed as a HMO; this was needed as there were large grey areas in the previous classification.

The Housing Act 2004 states that if there are three or more non-related people living in a property, whether they are on one tenancy agreement or three, the property will be classed as an HMO (house in multiple occupation) and therefore special rules apply.

This means that certain criteria are required to ensure that the property is safe to occupy. You will need to speak to your local council with regard to their specific criteria. Most local councils will release a booklet on the subject, explaining these clearly.

'Non-related' means people who do not form a 'household' and does not refer solely to people who are not related by blood. A same-sex couple, for example, would still constitute one household, so you need to specify your tenants' relationships on the tenancy agreement if ever there may be any room for doubt.

What does this mean?

This means that a house let to three or more non-related people will need to be amended to meet the needs of the number of people residing on the premises as the local council have stipulated.

Generally most of the changes required are with regard to fire safety. Your local council will have a document that can usually be downloaded from their website or a booklet you can collect with regard to HMO properties. Bringing a typical three-bed semi up to the regulations for an HMO can cost in the region of £10,000+, so be wary.

If you are letting a standard three-bed semi to a group of three people sharing, this will constitute an HMO property (non-licensable) and may require a mains Grade D fire system, thumb latches on all doors, half-hour fire-resistant doors throughout, self-closing devices on all doors, fire doors in the kitchens, a specific number of electric points in each of the bedrooms, a specific square footage of communal areas and bedrooms and the correct number of washing and toilet facilities, to name a few. This can be very costly.

The problem here lies in the fact that when you re-let the property it may be to a normal family and many of the changes will be redundant.

Licensing

Not all HMO properties have to be licensed.

Generally, a licensable HMO will be three or more storeys high and have five or more unrelated people sharing (not in self-contained flats). However, this can currently vary across councils' jurisdictions. Many councils have taken up their right to enforce additional licensing requirements in their local areas.

Some councils have also elected certain areas to come under Article 4, which means in some areas (generally poor or student areas) any person wishing to set up an HMO property would need to get planning consent to do so first.

If you are buying a property in an elected Article 4 zone, or you intend to have seven or more unrelated occupants in the house, then you will need to apply to change the use for the dwelling from C3 (family use) to C4 (unrelated people sharing).

If you are buying or converting a property into an HMO it is extremely important to check with your local council as to what their local guidelines are or are going to be, and to understand fully the steps you need to take. Falling foul of the licensing rules could leave you with a £20,000 fine amongst other potential penalties.

If your property qualifies to be licensed, then you will need to make an application to the council for a licence. Some councils will require you to attend a council-run course and pay a fee.

Once this is done the council will inspect your property to ensure that it is up to current standards and may insist on certain changes to be carried out. You will be given a timescale for getting these changes done.

Failure to comply with these regulations can result in prosecution. Some of the first test cases are coming out now and landlords who have not licensed their HMO properties have faced heavy fines as well as the tenants being entitled to one year's rent being re-paid to them.

Some landlords have faced jail sentences when tenants have been hurt as a result of lack of adequate safety measures, so ensure your property is safe and compliant.

Buildings that are excluded

Certain buildings or parts of buildings are not considered houses in multiple occupation, as detailed in Schedule 14 of the Housing Act 2004.

These include buildings that are managed or controlled by public sector bodies, buildings that are student-occupied and controlled by certain educational establishments, buildings that are regulated by other legislation, buildings that are occupied by religious communities, buildings that are occupied by their owners and household, and buildings that are occupied by two people.

HMO by declaration

If a local housing authority is confident that a building or part of a building in their locality is an HMO, they might serve a notice named 'HMO declaration' that confirms the building or part of a building to be a house in multiple occupation. The property must be occupied by people who don't form a single household.

HMOs in blocks of flats that have been converted

'Flats that have been converted' are a building or part of a building that has been converted into self-contained flats. Properties that are in a converted block of flats will be HMOs if:

- Less than two thirds of the self-contained flats are owner-occupied.

- Building work that has been done with regards to the conversion does not comply with the Building Regulations 1991. This will be the case if building work was completed before the regulations came into effect on the 1st June 1992.

Suitability tests for multiple occupation

The LHA won't be satisfied that a house is suitable for occupation by a certain maximum number of people or households, if it is seen that it would fail to meet with the prescribed standards for occupation by that number of people or households. 'Prescribed standards' describes the standards that have been prescribed by the regulations. These consist of:

- Standards for the type, quantity and quality of equipment or facilities that should be available.

- Standards for the type, quantity and quality of toilets, bathrooms, showers, washbasins and laundry facilities that should be available.

- Standards for the type, quantity, quality and size of rooms and food preparation areas that should be available.

The local authority will look to ensure the following things:

- The proposed management arrangements for the property are satisfactory.

- The property is suitable for occupation by the maximum number of persons or households specified, or it can be made suitable by the imposition of specific conditions.

- The proposed property manager is a proper and suitable person to be managing the property.

- The proposed licence holder is a proper and suitable person to be the licence holder.

- The proposed manager of the property is the person who has control of the house or an employee or agent of the person who has control of the house.

Conditions for a licence

A licence could include some conditions that the local housing authority deem suitable for regulating the management, occupation, condition and use of the property and its contents. These conditions might include:

- Prohibitions or restrictions for the occupation or use of certain parts of the house by the persons occupying it.

- Reasonable steps to be taken to reduce or prevent any anti-social behaviour by the persons who reside in or are visiting the property.

- Equipment and facilities to be made available in the property and to meet the prescribed standards within a specified period.

- Any such facilities to be kept in good repair and working order.

- Manager or licence holder to attend training courses regarding any codes of practice that are applicable.

A licence needs to include these requirements:

- To give the occupiers of the house a written tenancy agreement.

- To provide a copy of the annual gas safety certificate and display it in a communal area.

- To keep safe any furniture or appliances in the property and give the authority written confirmation of the safety of the furniture and appliances.

- To make sure that smoke alarms have been installed on the property, to provide the authority with written confirmation of the positioning and condition of the alarms, and to ensure these alarms are kept in proper working order and fitted to the appropriate grade.

Under the selective licensing provisions, a licence needs to include conditions requesting the licence holder to insist on references from the people who want to occupy the property.

Enforcement

A person will be committing an offence if:

- He is a licence holder or someone on whom restrictions or obligations are imposed by a licence, and fails to adhere to the licensing conditions.

- He is managing or has control of an HMO that has to be licensed, but is not in fact licensed.

- He is managing or has control of an HMO that is licensed, but purposely permits another person to reside in the property and exceeds the licensed occupation limit.

There are defences for these; they include having a genuine reason for giving permission for a person to occupy the property, or for failing to comply with the condition.

Someone who commits an offence will become liable for a summary conviction that carries a maximum fine of £20,000. A payment of rent cannot be enforced for an HMO that is unlicensed, and a residential property tribunal could make a 'rent repayment order' that requests that the appropriate person pay the applicant an amount with regard to the rent paid.

No Section 21 notice can be used to seek possession of all or part of a licensable HMO as long as it remains unlicensed.

Minimum facilities and amenities in HMOs

These are the national minimum standards, but local schemes might provide higher requirements for shared facilities. Landlord and agents need to check this with their local authorities. Other authorities have been asked to co-operate in keeping up comparable standards, but differences are sure to happen.

If the accommodation does not have individual toilet and bathing facilities for each sharer, there will need to be at least:

- A bathroom with a bath or a shower that has constant hot and cold water for every five occupants.

- Where appropriate, a separate toilet that has a sink with a tiled splashback for every five occupants.

- Fixed taps that supply hot and cold water for all sinks and baths.

If the standards set above are not met currently, the local authority will request changes to the property to meet these demands, unless the HMO is considered unsuitable for occupation by the proposed number of people. Also:

- All toilets and bathrooms must be located in a suitable place in the living accommodation.

- All toilets and bathrooms must have an appropriate layout and size.

- All toilets, baths and sinks must be fit for their purpose.

If the accommodation does not have exclusive cooking facilities for each sharer, there needs to be at least:

- A suitably-located kitchen with a reasonable layout and size, so that the persons occupying the accommodation can cook, prepare and store food.

- Extractor fans, fire doors and fire blankets fitted in the kitchen.

- A certain minimum level of equipment in the kitchen: cookers, electrical sockets, kettles, draining boards, and sinks with hot and cold water. Work surfaces for food preparation, fridges with freezer compartments, cupboards and refuse facilities. All of this must be fit for purpose.

Precautions for fire

Equipment that will satisfy the local fire service should be provided in the communal areas, including hallways, landings and kitchens, as appropriate.

Bedsits

These need to have facilities for washing and for preparing, cooking and storing food; there should be a kettle and a fridge. The bedsit must have space heating and include access to a toilet and bathing facilities.

Recommended actions for HMO or bedsit owners

- Keep records of all checks or works that have been carried out and any certificates given.

- Contact the council to find out more about their HMO registration scheme and if you would need to register. Forms should be completed ASAP, as some local authorities will charge for the time they take to process.

- Test emergency lighting every six months and equipment on a yearly basis to ensure good practice.

- Regular fire alarm tests should be done and an annual inspection organised with a qualified engineer.

- Regular testing should be carried out on all self-closing doors and devices.

- An annual inspection should be arranged for alarms, fire extinguishers or any other fire safety equipment.

To summarise

Lettings law:

- Get gas, electrical and fire safety certificates to show compliance. Gas certificates are absolutely compulsory.

- Ensure you use the correct agreements and don't contradict statutory law.

- Use the correct notice to gain possession.

- Keep your tenant safe.

- Understand your requirements under the HMO rules.

How to Find and Manage Your Letting Agent

How good is the agent at marketing properties?

- Does the agent have a good click-through rate on property portals? Do they display photos?

One of the initial and fundamental jobs for any letting agent is to let your property fast! Without a tenant, there will be no rent or management to do anyway, so it is of key importance to get this right. It is so common, though, for agents to get the marketing of properties horribly wrong. Quite often the person to whom the job of uploading the properties has been delegated is a junior or has not been long in the role and doesn't devote enough care and attention to this important task, or simply has not been trained to do so.

How good or bad the photos and description of the property are will affect the click-through rate that an online advert gets, in turn affecting the number of enquiries and therefore viewings. Thankfully for landlords, it is very easy to check up on an agent before you use them.

Check to see how many photos the agent has for each property. I would like to see two for each room along with a good front view and a garden view. Also look at the descriptions; are they clear and do they 'sell' the property, focusing on its best features and local facilities? They should not be too basic and must also not be misleading.

You will need great photos, preferably taken on a good light day. Ensure the property is tidy, the garden is as good as it can be, bins are tidy or out of view, and all curtains are pulled back tidily. Ideally there should be no cars parked in front. If there is snow on the ground, take photos, but go back and take more very soon after the snow has gone.

Descriptions should be detailed and list ALL the benefits of a property; even if that is only the close proximity of the bus route, it should all be there.

So when looking to take on an agent, look through the properties they have listed on their chosen property portal. See if ALL their properties have good-quality photos, both external and internal, and check the descriptions. When you have instructed an agent, it's also good to keep an eye on the portal and ensure that your property is uploaded in satisfactory time, not weeks!

- Does the agent deal with properties similar to yours?

Agents come in all types, and have various specialities. The type of property they advertise and work with will dictate the type of tenant they have on their lists, and the type of management system they have in the background.

Managing a portfolio of student lets is very different to managing a portfolio of professionals or LHA tenants, so it does make sense to go to an agent that has similar properties to yours on the books already.

- Does the agent take down the details of tenants who call?

Why not try them out with a tenant call? Tenants are the lifeblood of any letting agency. Let's face it: without any tenants, they are not going to do very well. If a busy agent records the details of all the tenants that they get calling, they should be registering well over 250 tenants a month onto their system. This means that when a property comes onto their books, they should already have someone on their books to take it!

However, so many agents do not take down tenant enquiries. I find this amazing; all that advertising to get the lead, just to throw it away ... but it happens. Some are just plain rude to tenants! So give them a call, posing as a tenant. How do they sound? Are they helpful and professional? Would you want to deal with them? Do they call you back? It's all a great test to see if the agent you are using or considering is doing a great job for you.

Is the agent qualified to do the job?

- Is the agent a member of ARLA/NAEA/RICS?

The lettings industry is still unregulated and, for this reason, anyone can set up as a letting agent with no training. Lettings and property management, however, are extremely complex areas, and a lot of expectation is on the agent to know what to do in a myriad of scenarios. Without training, an agent can fail to comply with regulations, and this can lead to fines for the landlord (even if responsibility has been delegated to the agent).

For this reason I feel it is extremely important to be sure that your agent has the backing of ARLA, NAEA or RICS. This way you can know that they have been trained and checked to make sure they do everything properly.

If your agent is a member of the above, you know that these regulatory bodies are checking their company set-up, indemnity insurance and client account bond, looking at their bank account balances to ensure the money is correctly apportioned, and ensuring the agent has at least one qualified person in the business at any time. The agent will have to abide by the bodies' strict codes of conduct throughout. They will also have to have Client Money Protection in place to protect any clients that may suffer a loss due to the closure of a branch etc.

There are other Client Money Protection covering bodies around, but this is not all that is required to protect you. Account auditing, qualifications and codes of conduct go way beyond merely checking that an insurance policy, which could easily be cancelled at any time, is in place.

- How many members of staff does the agent have and what do they all do?

Understaffing is a key indicator of underservice. If an agent tells you that they have 500 properties under management and only one property manager, then you know that there will be problems. In the industry, the average staff-to-property ratio is around 75 properties per staff member, so count the staff and find out how many properties they are actually managing.

When a company is understaffed, it means that a lot of the services you might have come to expect just won't be done. Calls may not be returned, maintenance not checked and arrears not jumped on, and this will lead to disgruntled clients all round.

- Does the agent specialise in lettings?

Make sure the company see lettings as a priority, not just a tag on to their 'main' business. Letting properties is hard work, and requires dedication from above to get it right. If the idea is that lettings will make a bit of revenue whilst sales in another area are low, then the systems and training needed to do the job properly will never be invested in and the clients will suffer through lack of professional service.

Referencing your agent

- Check the agent out!

Many landlords spend a lot of time and resources checking out their tenants, but in two decades of lettings I have never been asked to provide landlord references on our agency. A bad letting agent can do as much damage to a landlord as a bad tenant can, if not more, especially if you have multiple proper-ties with them.

When considering using a letting agent, I would definitely look online for reviews. Just type in the letting agency's name and 'reviews' into a search engine, such as Google, and you will see what comes up, good and bad. Then ask the agency for some current clients to talk to who have been with them for some time.

This should give you a real flavour of what you will experience.

The appraisal: the clues are all there!

How much information does the agent give?

The appraisal is a key meeting. At the appraisal or valuation, you should expect to get some real key advice from the agent. They should be looking to explain to you the current market and where your property sits within that, any works required at the property and why, any health and safety risks to attend to, and how to optimise your returns on that property by maybe looking at alternative tenancy types or doing works to the property to raise the rent level.

However, unfortunately, many agents merely give you a valuation and walk away, not feeling they can give a landlord 'honest' advice for fear that this will scare them away. If you feel an agent is in a hurry, or just telling you what you want to hear, then maybe look a bit further.

- What's the agent's knowledge of the area and market? Do you know more than them?

You are going to an agent because you want their expertise. The valuation is an opportunity for them to demonstrate this expertise in the local market to you. How do you feel about them? Do they know more than you? Do you feel safe with them? Could they answer your questions? Do you know more for having met them? Be honest with yourself; you may like them, but can you trust them to know what to do when you have the tenant from hell in your house?

- What's their back office support?

The business of lettings is complex and 24-hour; any letting agent needs a back office support of some type. Do they have an online computer system for back-up, do they have a management department or team, have they got out-of-hours calls, or do they really answer the phone at all hours of the day and night? Do they have a team of contractors, colleagues, experienced directors, head office support? What would happen if they left or went on holiday?

The real test: paperwork!

- 'It's OK; my agent deals with all that!'

Many people take on an agent and then feel, 'I don't have to worry about that now; the agent will take care of it!'

If it is a good agent they are right, but unfortunately in law, you as the landlord are still responsible if the agent gets it wrong. In the early days of using an agent, keep an eye on things.

Check your tenancy files to ensure that all the documents (the inventory, the tenancy agreement etc.) are signed, that the gas certificate is present and that the references have been done satisfactorily. Keep track of when your gas certificate is due and ensure you get copies. Keep an eye on when your rent is paid and pay close attention if it becomes overdue, to ensure your agent is dealing with any arrears.

Since the Localism Act 2011, it is now crucially important to make sure that your deposit is registered within 30 days of receiving it. If you have delegated this to the agent, you need to be checking in the early days to make sure that they have registered the deposit and sent you and the tenants a copy of the paperwork.

To summarise

- Test your agent's marketing potential.

- Check their qualifications; are they experienced?

- Take references and check the agent's set-up.

- At the appraisal, test the agent's knowledge.

- Take a look at the paperwork!

In Conclusion

Being a landlord can sometimes feel like a thankless task, but most tenants really appreciate a nice clean and safe home. With so many people now turning to the private rented sector through choice rather than necessity, it is even more important to work with your tenants and run your property portfolio as a business and treat your tenants as 'clients' or customers.

Property investment is a great tool for building assets to secure your future, but in the meantime it has to operate successfully and with as little hassle as possible, whilst generating the cash you need.

By following the processes in this book, you will come to know the key points to consider when letting and managing a property yourself, the main regulations and safety issues you need to bear in mind, and how to deal with letting agents.

My team of agents make it their goal to take the pain away from renting property, and in the main, with good processes and systems, this is easy to do. Get it right first time and every time, then the rest is easy.

Simple!

Answer to 'Which law would you break?'

Neither. After trying to make appointments, offering to go in with keys and writing to the tenant telling them you will go in on a particular date (to which on all occasions they have called up your office and refused to let you in), you would need to seek access through the courts or issue notice on the tenant if possible.

Contributed Chapters

Andy Halstead: Managing Risk

All investments have risk and residential property is no exception. Property values rise and fall and the income from the investment is at risk; this can be particularly problematic if the property investment has a mortgage debt. Whilst it is not possible to remove risk entirely, it is possible for landlords to manage the risk and reduce the risk exposure to nothing more than extreme circumstances.

Managing risk starts at the initial investment stage; engaging in a thorough due diligence process before purchasing the property is essential. The following questions need to be answered satisfactorily:

- Do you know the area where the property is located?

- What have the property price trends been during the last ten years?

- Does the RICS valuation stack up to recent sales of similar properties in the area?

- What is the demand for rental properties in the area?

- What have at least three independent letting agents valued the rental income at?

- How long do similar properties take to rent?

If the above questions are answered satisfactorily and backed up with solid data, then the investment process is off to a good start.

The compliance and regulatory risk faced by landlords is significant. From gas certificates and EPCs to legally binding contracts and tenancy agreements, the risks and potential penalties can result in hefty fines, even prison sentences. Appointing a professional letting agent is essential, and again due diligence in this process is very important:

- Is the potential letting agent ARLA/NALS/Safe Agent registered?

- How long has the letting agent been trading?

- Take at least three references from landlords who use the letting agent's services.

- Does the letting agent offer professional tenant referencing, rent guarantee and legal protection?

- Does the letting agent have a quality website and also market all properties on Rightmove, Zoopla etc.?

- Does the letting agent have a quality high-street presence?

- Have you met the letting agent business owner?

If the answers to the above questions are satisfactory and backed up with robust data and evidence, then appointing a professional letting agent will mitigate risk; in fact much of the compliance and regulatory risk is transferred to the letting agent. Make sure that the contact between the landlord and the agent reflects the risk transfer.

Tenant selection and assessment is a crucial process in the mitigation of risk; the asset value of the property and the monthly yield is dependent upon a quality, suitable tenant being selected to take up the tenancy agreement. The following tenant checks are essential:

- Last three years' address history.

- Financial checks, including payment history records.

- Employer references, including a statement about earnings and job security.

- Previous landlord references, including a statement about how the property was looked after.

- Affordability calculation.

- Guarantors whenever required, fully referenced.

- A minimum one month's deposit available and the first month's rent available to be paid in advance.

- A detailed description of the potential tenants' circumstances; children/pets/smokers.

Tenants also face risk. Even the very best tenants can fall on difficult times through no fault of their own. Illness, divorce, job loss etc. can materially affect the tenant's ability to pay the rent. This risk can be entirely illuminated through the purchase of a nil excess rent guarantee policy that pays the rent in full from the first day of arrears until either the tenant pays or vacant possession is obtained. Rent guarantee protection also covers the full cost of legal expenses, so the rental income is secure. This is particularly important when a landlord has a mortgage on the property, along with service charges that must be paid, even when the tenant defaults.

Residential property can be a secure, high-yielding investment. The costs associated with managing risk have a positive effect on the yield. When the risk management is thorough, void periods are minimised, rent is guaranteed, fines associated with non-compliance are avoided and the property is well managed, optimising the asset value.

Throughout the term of each tenancy, it is crucial that the letting agent carries out quarterly property inspections, and produces a detailed report and updated inventory following each inspection. This activity will identify problem tenants who might well be paying the rent in full and on time each month. It is the role of a professional letting agent to minimise costs relating to general maintenance and repairs. Early intervention when a tenant is abusing the property is essential.

Finally, specialist landlord buildings and contents insurance, with nil excess wherever possible, will protect the investor against a whole range of risks, in addition to the obvious fire and theft major perils, including:

- Malicious damage by the tenant.

- Cost of accommodation for the tenant should the property be uninhabitable.

- Landlord's liability.

Specialist insurance can also offer full insurance protection during void periods and can cover the cost of emergency call-out and emergency repairs.

Landlords should also insist that tenants have valid tenants' liability insurance. This protects the landlord should the tenant damage goods belonging to the landlord. Again, whenever possible, this insurance should carry no excess.

The costs incurred when managing risk are fully tax-deductible for landlords resident in the United Kingdom. 'Net yield' will be maximised and capital value of the property will be optimised if landlords follow the risk management advice in this article. Shortcuts and ignoring the risks almost always result in unexpected, high costs that severely damage the performance of residential investment property.

Andy Halstead
Founder of Let Alliance

Let Alliance was established in 2011 to serve the UK letting agent marketplace. Founder Andy Halstead and the senior management team have extensive industry experience. From 2004 to 2008 Andy and his senior team led the Barbon businesses Homelet, Letsure and Rentshield.

Let Alliance is different, specialising in exclusively working with letting agents. The business has experienced exponential growth since launch. From a desk and a telephone above their letting agency business in Chester, Let Alliance has now expanded to work with more than 1,000 letting agency firms. The Let Alliance proposition is based on team and customer; everything that they do enhances the customer experience. Tenant referencing is the core competency of Let Alliance and this supports their ability to offer the best rent guarantee, legal expenses and 'Right to Rent' protection in the marketplace. Currently no other tenant referencing provider warrants the letting agent against any penalties should they fall foul of the Immigration Bill and Right to Rent legislation.

Let Alliance offers an account manager relationship proposition, not a call centre administration proposition that so often frustrates customers. Let Alliance is about people and relationships. Customers are never asked to enter into contractual terms; however, the customer relationships are long-term.

Let Alliance is passionate about letting agents and believes that landlords should work with letting agents rather than self-manage. Professional letting agents offer a great service and real value for money. Let Alliance supports letting agents in managing risk on behalf of landlord and tenant customers.

Let Alliance is independently owned and works strategically with DAS and UKGI. Let Alliance has full delegated authority and is regulated by the FCA.

Andy Halstead has an extensive and successful track record in sales and growing businesses, from board positions at blue-chip firms Prudential, AMP and AIG to start-up businesses Lomond Capital LLP, Rent on Time Ltd and Let Alliance Ltd. Andy specialises in growth through sales and marketing; he has also led more than 30 business acquisitions.

For the last ten years Andy has focused on the private rental sector in the UK and in addition to his CEO position at Let Alliance, Andy is a partner at Lomond Capital LLP, Chairman at Jordan Halstead Properties Ltd and Chairman at Rent on Time Ltd. A passionate believer in people and teams, Andy has a leadership style that focuses on the business strategy and allows team members to get on with what they do best, delivering a world-class customer experience.

Married with four grown-up children and one granddaughter, Andy lives in Chester. A Manchester United supporter and holder of a season ticket at Manchester City: complicated ... Andy's son Jordan is a lifelong blue.

Nick Carlile: Fundamentals of Property Investing

I started investing in property in 1993. Now, for those of you saying that it was easy to make money back then and you can't do this now, I would totally disagree.

Firstly, when I bought the house in 1993 at the age of 19 most people were saying similar things and telling me I was absolutely mad.

Unemployment was very high across the UK, interest rates had been as high as 15% and repossessions were still extremely common. The economy had major uncertainty running through it and the property market had just recently been corrected from some very high prices. Indeed, there was an overwhelming feeling that prices just couldn't recover again.

The comments were along the lines of 'the market has recently crashed and there is no way it's going to rise again', 'just look at all the people that have been repossessed', 'interest rates are still volatile', 'you must be mad to buy now' and my old favourite, 'it's got much further to fall'.

In today's market through our property investment business we hear the same comments from time to time. For the record I do agree that there is still some volatility in the market and the wider world, but overwhelming demand for property and the massive shortage of supply are just two of the main reasons why we believe that property prices will rise again in the future. This is also the backbone of our belief that property is an extremely safe long-term investment.

The principles which we adopt in our property investment strategy give excellent security against such volatility.

We call these the **Five Fundamentals of Property Investing** and they are explained in more detail in our annual Guide to Property Investing, which we offer free to anyone who wants a copy.

These five fundamentals are:

- Always buy at a discount.

- Always add value.

- Ensure that the property is cashflow positive.

- Always invest for the medium to long term.

- Stack the odds in your favour.

These five fundamentals are the backbone of our current business where we build property portfolios for our clients who want to invest in a hands-free manner.

I realise now that in my early investing I was adopting some (not all) of these principles and it was this that made me successful rather than just the market or my skills as a QS.

Those early lessons of buying at a discount and adding value ensured that, whatever the market was doing, I had some significant protection. They also ensured that I was positioned with a property investment portfolio for when the market started to race upwards again.

Knowing what I know now, I wish I'd bought much more property in those early years. We hear this all the time from people who are waiting for the perfect time to invest. The fact is that there is no perfect time to invest in property, but, in our opinion: **the only bad time to buy property is later**.

In reality there are four factors which need to align in order for prices to rise again significantly.

We call them the **Four Factors for Growth** and they are:

1. Supply and demand.

In any market for any product, the law of supply and demand is one of the major factors in how prices react.

Put simply: when demand is greater than supply, prices will rise. When supply is greater than demand, prices will fall.

This is a given when it comes to the UK property market, because we have such a shortage of housing. Supply simply doesn't keep up with demand, and this problem isn't being fixed by any of the governments who try.

Add to this that we live on a tiny island with a growing population, restrictive planning laws and a culture where people want to buy rather than rent, and you have an ever-buoyant demand for property.

This in turn ensures that prices will always rise over the long term. Yes, we have peaks and troughs but the long term is always upwards.

2. Affordability.

This is an important factor, because even with significant demand, people need to be able to afford to buy their homes.

In the run-up to the credit crunch the normal rules of banking were ignored by many lenders in relation to mortgage afford-ability. Instead of checking your bank balance and your employment, many lenders just checked if you had a pulse. If you did, you could have a mortgage.

The lenders of old used to lend you around three times your salary on a mortgage. During the period leading up to the credit crunch, some lenders introduced 'self-certified mortgages'. These were mortgages where you didn't have to prove any income and the lenders would simply believe what you told them.

Add this to the fact that they then started to lend at higher multiples of your income, and affordability during those times wasn't an issue.

Many overstretched themselves and it's only the drop in base rate to an all-time low that saved, and still is saving, many investors and homeowners from financial ruin.

It was the unaffordability of property which was one of the key factors in the correction of house prices in the UK.

Now that the lenders have regained their senses (or maybe the FSA/FCA have forced them to), affordability is very important.

Since the credit crunch, property has become much more afford-able in many areas, although you can forget London and large parts of the South East.

It's this affordability that is bringing more people to the table to buy property. This in turn will create further demand, which in turn will cause prices to rise again over the medium to long term.

You can look at Nationwide's affordability indices to see how affordable property is in any area, available at:

www.nationwide.co.uk/about/house-price-index/download-data

3. Finance.

As mentioned above in point 2, the majority of lenders were astonishingly keen to lend in the run-up to the credit crunch.

Immediately after the credit crunch they all withdrew and it was virtually impossible for anyone to raise finance for property.

Since that time, and over the past six years, finance has slowly returned to the market and indeed we have seen the creation of some completely new lenders.

Whilst these lenders are much stricter than the pre-credit-crunch days, the return of finance to the market is another factor which will see demand rise and therefore prices rise again over the medium to long term.

4. Confidence.

This is perhaps the most important of the Four Factors for Growth.

Even if you have high demand, affordability and finance: if the press are telling stories of doom and gloom, risk and adversity, people won't go out and spend their money. They will hunker down and wait for the storm to pass.

In the aftermath of the credit crunch all the press talked about was how doomed we all were. How Europe was going to collapse. How big the deficit was. How stupid the banks had been to lend all that money. And how stupid we had all been to borrow it.

It's only really since the start of 2014 that we have started to see a lot more positivity in the press, which in turn has given more confidence to the general public to start their love affair with property again.

These Four Factors for Growth are never perfectly aligned, but right now they are close to perfect. You could wait another few years and be one of those people who look back and say, 'I wish I'd bought more property back then when it was cheaper.'

The current circumstances which we face – the position of the market, the lack of competition, the massive undersupply of property, rising rents, cheap finance – mean that it's a great time to invest. It's actually land grab time, similar to all the other times when the market cycle has been in a similar position to now.

The fact that the majority of people believe that finance is more difficult to obtain (many people think impossible) is a good thing as it keeps a lot of the competition away. This makes it a buyers' market and drives the significant discounts of 20–40% that we achieve on every property which we buy.

Circumstances are very similar to when I started to invest, in that the majority of people are fearful of investing and a handful of people are quietly building investment portfolios.

> *Buy when others are selling and sell when others are buying.*
> Warren Buffett, the second-richest man in the world
> (you would think he knows his stuff).

It feels like a second chance to invest and to position myself and our clients with significant investments ready for when the market turns again.

This is what we believe in and we are helping others maximise the opportunity that exists and may not exist again for another 20–30 years.

Do you want to wait for the next cycle to come around before you take advantage of such excellent timing to invest?

If you need more convincing, here are 13 compelling reasons to invest in property.

1. Traditional pension systems are not enough.

There are lots of reasons why I believe the traditional pension systems fail – not least why there are a lot more people taking out than the number that are paying in. Whichever party is in power, whatever your political stance, that's going to be a problem for them.

I'd like to share with you the main reason why I bought my first house back in 1993 and my main reason for writing this now. It stems from my dad who, like millions of others, had paid into a pension and received around half of what he thought he should have received.

Imagine working for over 40 years of your life.

Imagine putting aside much of your disposable income and forgoing many of the day-to-day pleasures in the hope that your retirement would be more secure and enjoyable.

Imagine the memory of all the times you told your kids that they couldn't have the new bike or the extra holiday because money was tight.

Imagine getting to retirement age and finding that the projections were so far off the mark that it's almost criminal.

Imagine getting to retirement age and finding that the pay-out was about half of what was projected.

Imagine looking back and thinking, *I wish I'd done something else back then. Anything else. Something in addition to my traditional pension. Even just a hedge in case the traditional stuff didn't perform.*

Imagine the feeling of it all being way too late.

Now is the time to do something about it. Now is the time to take action. If not in property, then in something, in anything as a hedge against a traditional pension provision.

    2. There is a fundamental shortage of housing in the UK.

When you boil it down to basics, most markets come down to simple supply and demand as we discussed earlier.

- There is only one David Beckham in the world and that's why he continues to command multi-million-pound transfer fees and wages, even in his late career.

- In this digital age the front page of Google is a fixed supply, in that there are only so many spaces on this front page. Demand for the front page is increasing and therefore so is the cost of ownership.

- Oil is still very difficult and expensive to harvest and has a reducing supply. Demand continues to increase throughout the world despite the best efforts of many with 'green' intentions.

A reducing supply and increasing demand will always see prices rise.

Property in the UK is still in short supply. The recent events of the excessive price rises in the early 2000s and the global financial crisis have skewed the natural market out of balance. Basic economics of supply and demand will, however, always win out and there is still and always will be a fundamental shortage of housing in the UK.

We are a tiny island and the fourth most densely populated country in Europe.

Our planning laws are some of the most restrictive in the world, meaning that our ability to build further homes is not matched by our desire to do so on our countryside.

We have a growing population. The 2011 census recorded the largest increase in population since records began in 1801. The Office for National Statistics estimates that the UK population will be as high as 70 million by 2027. This is an increase of around 438,000 per year, or a city the size of Bristol. That's an astounding amount of growth and a major problem for the UK housing market.

We simply aren't building enough homes to keep pace with demand. The recent study by the Future Homes Commission called for 300,000 new homes to be built every year, to keep up with demand. We are currently only building around 100,000 per year.

For years we built the wrong types of accommodation. Those one- and two-bedroom apartments in city centres were all the rage in the early to mid 2000s. It seemed that every town and city was overrun with them and in a lot of cases there is still a massive oversupply. Many of those developments are empty, bought by novice investors who wanted to ride the wave of UK property, but who sadly invested in the wrong type of property.

We are a great country with liberal policies on immigration. We positively welcome immigration and this has created the wonderfully diverse culture that we enjoy in the UK today. This has contributed to the growth in population and with it the growing shortage of housing.

Because of the word count restrictions of the book I've listed below the items from 3 to 13. Simply drop me an email for a free report which contains the complete list in full detail.

3. Everyone needs (WANTS) a place to live.

4. Property has always risen in value over time since records began.

5. The eighth wonder of the world – leverage.

6. Capital growth and cash flow.

7. You can add value to property.

8. The rental sector is booming and will continue to do so.

9. Finance is relatively easy when compared to other investments and businesses.

10. The property market is a predictable cycle and you can profit from this boom and bust.

11. You can keep score and make substitutions (to use a sporting analogy).

12. There are significant tax advantages to property ownership.

13. You can be an active or passive investor.

Nick Carlile
Managing Director and Property Entrepreneur
www.platinumportfoliobuilder.co.uk
nick@platinumportfoliobuilder.co.uk
01226 732 606

Nick loves property! It's often been said that if he was chopped in half, PROPERTY would run through him like a stick of rock. From the moment he stepped out of school and onto a building site, at the age of 16, he was enraptured with every element of the property business, from the actual building works, the budgeting and surveying through to the deals themselves.

Having seen his father work hard all his life only to get a tiny pension at the end of it, Nick believed that investing in property offered a better alternative. He has since proved this youthful suspicion right, buying his first house aged just 19 in 1993 and then continuing to buy, build, and invest into property in every year since then. Nick's portfolio now consists of enough property to provide a solid retirement plan, which was his goal from the start.

A qualified surveyor, today Nick continues to buy, renovate, build and manage an expanding number of carefully selected properties in the north of England. In doing this, he has transformed half a lifetime's experience in property, insight and business aptitude into a £40 million property portfolio, mostly on behalf of investor clients.

When he's not investing in, looking at or writing about property, Nick loves to warm up for the Great North Run, which he completes each year for charity. He has also completed the London Marathon, scaled the three peaks and climbed Mont Blanc.

Richard Bowser: Preparing for the Robotic Takeover

You will probably be reading this book because you are either thinking of buying property to let to tenants or you already a buy-to-let residential landlord. In which case you are also a property investor!

Whatever your aims and aspiration, you need to understand one thing about property investment: it can completely transform your long-term wealth prospects if you make the right decisions, at the right time. Every week I personally meet and speak with individuals who have created significant wealth from property investment, often having started out with quite modest funds. Is it easy? No, of course not, and although there can be some 'quick wins' along the way, investing in property is mostly a 'get rich slow' process.

However, in the twelve years that we have been publishing *Property Investor News* magazine I have seen so many individuals make huge mistakes with property investing, all too often because they treat it with an 'amateur' attitude. If you are serious about growing a long-term property portfolio and perhaps also becoming a property developer then you will only succeed if you adopt a professional attitude.

In comparison to early 2001, the world we know has been transformed by the information technology revolution and we now have 24/7 access via our fingertips on PDAs and mobile phones. The problem is that there is so much 'disinformation' out there and some of that 'advice/knowledge' is quite dangerous for those who are just starting out with property investment.

Marketers who want to 'sell the sizzle' will present investing strategies to new investors which can appear quite straightforward and compelling. Unfortunately the reality behind some of the 'fashionable' property-investing strategies is that there is no substitute for hard graft, and careful due diligence when sourcing investment property is really important.

And it's no different when sourcing tenants; you and/or your letting agent will make the choice of tenant, but all too often landlords will accept the first person who agrees the asking rent and this can lead on to a costly and stressful experience. So don't become one of those who 'act in haste and repent at leisure'.

Take your time when choosing property and tenants; think carefully about which investing strategies you want to adopt. Even if you only have one or two properties, think and act with a professional mindset and really focus on what you want to achieve with your property-investing activities.

Just as with the information technology revolution, the world is changing fast and as a property investor/landlord you need to think ahead and position your investments to maximise rental income and capital growth. Whether you are letting to student tenants, professional workers or to low-income 'social housing' tenants you can be sure of one thing: the way we live and work is evolving rapidly due to technological change. As such I trust the following will help you in understanding why you need think carefully about where and what properties you buy or sell in the years ahead.

Automation – it could take your job but could it also devalue your house?

Advances in technology are drastically changing the employment market and things could get worse before they get better.

I eventually wake up at 7am. My smartphone app has been 'gently waking me up' for the past ten minutes. I instantly smell the coffee that has just brewed itself as requested when I set the timer last night. As I leave my house I hear a rummaging sound from behind my neighbour's fence. I realise it is his robotic lawnmower quietly finishing off another night shift … his lawn looks perfect. I wonder how long it will be until a robot can trim my hedge …

Driving to work, Spotify (on my phone) randomly selects all my favourite music and plays it through the car stereo. I have not listened to the radio for months. I fill up my car at the fully automated petrol station, then drive through the automated car-wash. I then go to the supermarket to buy some milk, withdrawing some cash from the hole in the wall outside … I have not set foot inside a bank for years. From the ten check-outs available at the supermarket, only one cashier is actually working. Nearly every customer uses the self-checkout to save time.

I am first to arrive at my office building but there is no longer any overnight security guard to say hello to. The alarm system is far too high-tech to worry about a break-in. At my desk, my computer shows me that 129 emails were received overnight; however, only 36 make it into my inbox. The rest have been dumped into 'junk' by my assistant – sorry, I mean computer – to save me more time. The first email I open is confirmation of the holiday that I booked online yesterday. I last went to a travel agent in the 1990s. I pause and laugh, remembering the film that I streamed from my iPad through my Apple TV last night. I have not rented a DVD for years ... no wonder Blockbusters went bust. It then occurs to me that I have only seen one person working all morning ... where have all the employees gone?

Just five years ago, half of the things described above would have felt more like a scene from a science fiction film. But it is now everyday life for many people. Technology is moving fast, but 'you ain't seen nothing yet'!

Just look at how supercomputing has progressed at IBM. In the nineties it focused its efforts on pure computation, eventually defeating chess champion Garry Kasparov. Then in 2011, its 'Watson' computer triumphed at *Jeopardy!* – the US game show that requires intuition as well as intelligence.

Now, IBM is repurposing Watson for human professions, such as medicine, law and even customer service. The line between man and machine is blurring beyond anything we could imagine even a few years ago.

However, while technology brings with it a number of benefits in our everyday lives, it has been replacing human workers for many decades. The question is not whether automation will eventually take your job (it will); it is whether enough of us will be able to find new jobs that computers can't do so that we can maintain, as a country, continent and a planet, a sizeable middle class. Should we fail to do so, and the middle class evaporate, leaving a few extremely wealthy business (and robot) owners and a huge majority of unemployed paupers, we all know what impact that would have on property prices. But will it happen?

The four types of employment

There are four types of job. These are primary, secondary, tertiary and quaternary jobs.

Primary jobs involve getting raw materials from the natural environment through mining, farming and fishing. Technological improvements have seen the number of people in the US working in primary jobs fall from 66% in 1850 to just 3% today.

Secondary jobs involve making things from raw materials (manufacturing) and for more than three decades, technology has reduced the number of jobs in manufacturing also. Robots and other machines work faster and make fewer mistakes than humans. Secondary jobs already lost include auto plant assembly workers. One robot, which can work around the clock, replaces the work of four humans, increasing productivity and decreasing costs.

Sixty years ago, factory jobs were a staple of life for workers in Europe and the US, and they employed nearly one-third of the workforce. While some jobs have been exported overseas, computerised machines have replaced the majority of them.

Tertiary jobs involve the selling of services and skills. Examples of tertiary employment include healthcare, transportation, education, entertainment, tourism, finance, sales and retail.

Although it was considered safe from automation for many years, that same efficiency is now being unleashed in the service economy, which employs more than two-thirds of the workforce in most developed countries, and 81% of workers in the UK.

Technology is eliminating jobs in office buildings, retail establishments and other businesses every single day.

This is where things start to get really ugly because the computer actually has the capacity to be more destructive to the service industry than it was to the industrial sector. This is because the pace at which it is upending industries makes it harder for people to adapt and retrain.

Automated telephone systems have replaced help desks, customer service operators and receptionists in many organisations. While it is still possible to speak to a human if you need assistance, these operators are shrinking in number each year.

Not all cashiers have been eliminated by technology yet, but the number of living cashiers is expected to decrease with the addition of more self-checkout equipment. In many supermarkets, there are more computer cashiers than human cashiers, and demand for self-checkout machines is soaring.

Finally, the *quaternary* sector consists of those industries providing information services, such as computing, ICT (information and communication technologies), consultancy (offering advice to businesses) and R&D (research, particularly in scientific fields). These jobs appear the most secure from automation ... for now.

The underemployed era

Global unemployment has now reached its highest level since the Great Depression of the 1930s. More than 800 million people are currently unemployed or underemployed in the world.

In the US, *Fortune* magazine found that corporations are eliminating more than 2 million jobs annually. Thanks to technology, companies listed on the S&P 500 stock index reported one-third more profit in 2012 than they earned the year before the Great Recession ... fewer workers equals more profits.

We are entering unknown territory in the quest to reduce labour costs. The AI revolution is doing to white-collar jobs what robotics did to blue-collar jobs. Most of these jobs will never return and millions more are likely to vanish.

'There's no sector of the economy that's going to get a pass,' Martin Ford, who runs a software company and wrote *The Lights in the Tunnel*, a book predicting widespread job losses, told the Associated Press. 'It's everywhere.'

Think travel agents, salespeople in stores, office assistants and back-office workers like payroll clerks, as well as machine operators and other factory jobs. An August 2012 paper by the University of British Columbia found these kinds of jobs comprise fewer than half of all jobs, yet accounted for nine out of ten of all losses in the recent Great Recession. And they have kept disappearing throughout the economic recovery.

In the US, half of the 7.5 million jobs lost during the Great Recession were in industries that pay middle-class wages, but only 2% of the 3.5 million jobs gained since the recession ended in June 2009 are in those mid-pay industries. Nearly 70% are low-paying jobs, while 29% are well-paid jobs.

In the Eurozone the numbers are even worse. Almost 4.3 million low-pay jobs were gained between mid-2009 and mid-2012, but the loss of mid-pay jobs has never stopped. A total of 7.6 million have disappeared from January 2008 through to mid-2012. Throughout the EU, the number of people unemployed has increased by 10 million (from 16 million to 26 million) over the past five years.

Experts warn that this 'hollowing out' of the middle-class workforce is far from over. They predict the loss of millions more jobs as technology becomes even more sophisticated.

Some occupations are beneficiaries of technology, such as software engineers and app designers for smartphones and tablet computers. Overall, though, technology is eliminating far more jobs than it is creating.

Start-ups account for much of the job growth in developed economies, but software is allowing entrepreneurs to launch businesses with a third fewer employees than they needed in the 1990s. There is less need for administrative support and back-office jobs that handle accounting, payroll and benefits.

More of the same in the future

Experts in the field of technology estimate that before the end of this century, 70% of today's occupations will be replaced by automation. In other words, robot replacement is just a matter of time.

First, fruit and vegetable picking will continue to be robotised until no humans pick outside specialty farms. Pharmacies will feature a single pill-dispensing robot in the back while the pharmacists focus on patient consulting. Next, tasks such as cleaning in offices and schools will be taken over by late-night robots, starting with easy-to-do floors and windows and eventually getting to toilets.

Machines will then consolidate their gains in already-automated industries. After robots finish replacing assembly line workers, they will replace the workers in warehouses. Speedy bots able to lift 100kg boxes all day long will sort them and load them onto trucks. Those trucks will drive to their destination ... by themselves.

Software is already running trains without drivers. The UAE introduced the world's longest automated rail system (32 miles) in Dubai in 2009. The trains on several Japanese rail lines are completely automated.

The Australian mining giant Rio Tinto started trials of driverless trucks in 2008 and in April 2013 the firm announced that its automated haul trucks had already moved more than 100 million tonnes of earth. By 2016 the mining industry will be highly automated with the bulk of entry-level jobs disappearing for good.

As the use of robots increases, mining will expand into new environments and locations that were previously off-limits to humans. This includes the seafloor, rich in metals like gold, copper and nickel. Longer-term plans are already being made to exploit asteroids.

Just as fracking is revolutionising the oil industry and has almost stopped the use of the term 'peak oil' in its tracks, automation used in the mining of all commodities will only point prices in one direction and that is downward, especially if the middle classes are not working as much and are therefore unable to buy new homes etc. Demand for commodities may not keep up with the increase in supply.

Closer to home, in November 2015 all trucks in the EU must be fitted with emergency braking systems, in effect making it impossible to crash them even if the driver falls asleep. By the end of this decade, that system will be extended to cars also. While it is obviously a huge positive that car accidents will be a thing of the past within the next ten years, these self-braking systems are a simple stepping stone to self-driving cars.

Driverless cars will have a revolutionary impact on traffic one day ... and on the job market. In the US alone, 3.1 million people drive trucks for a living, 573,000 drive buses and 342,000 drive taxis or limousines. All those jobs will be threatened by automated vehicles. Google and Toyota are already rolling out cars that can drive themselves.

Soon garbage collection will be completely automated. In the US alone, over 4 million driving and driving-related jobs are in danger of being lost. These job losses alone would push the US unemployment rate up by another 2.8%, or increase the number of unemployed by 37%!

If automation can unseat bus drivers, urban deliverymen (Domino's Pizza has already started testing its 'pizza drone', which it is calling a 'DomiCopter'), long-haul truckers and even cabbies, is any job safe?

Picture an investment banker in a bar on a Friday night with a smug look upon his face as he gulps down expensive champagne and boasts about how much he has earned that week. He no doubt thinks he deserves such exorbitant bonuses because he is a genius of sorts ... well, his job is likely to be taken by automation also. Computer software can already spot stock-market movements and make profits from stock trades in milliseconds. Why on earth will Goldman Sachs dilute their profits in the near future, by paying high salaries to bankers, when a computer can do a better job ... for free?

But my job is obviously safe. No computer can compete with the creative (self-declared genius) mind of an experienced journalist ... oh no, wait ... a piece of software designed by Narrative Science can already write newspaper stories about sports games directly from the games' stats, or generate a synopsis of a company's stock performance each day from bits of text around the web.

That's not all. An app is already on the market that allows novelists to have their work auto-corrected/copy-edited in the style of William Shakespeare or Charles Dickens. How long until all magazines can be auto-corrected by a Stephen Fry app? Once that is possible, a magazine editor could pay a freelance writer in India or China to research and write an article at a fraction of the price, Google translate it into English, then have it perfectly auto-corrected ... a decade or so later and no human will be needed to create articles, as software will do it all for you. You will simply tell the computer your interests and it will produce a tailor-made newspaper for you every day. Oops!

UK job losses

However, it is when we look at retail jobs in the UK that automation begins to look even scarier. The retail industry employs 2.8 million people in the UK and is the UK's largest private sector employer. The current UK retail market is dominated by a comparatively small number of large retailers who have 500+ employees. These large retailers employ 66% of all people working in retail. It is the large retailers that will embrace automation first, having the resources available to buy the machines and to use nanotechnology to carefully monitor every item. It is likely that from the current 1.8 million employed in retail in the UK by these large retail firms at least 1 million jobs could be lost to automation over the next ten years. This alone would increase the number of unemployed people in the UK by almost one-third!

Logistics employs more than 2 million people in the UK, while almost 5 million people work in business and administration. Half a million people are employed in private security services, but soon no human will be able to compete with a robot that can sense the increased heart rate of a thief or scan a thousand faces in seconds searching for a terrorist.

More than 2.35 million people work in the construction industry in the UK, with 40% being skilled trades like electricians, carpenters and plumbers. How long until a robot can fit a carpet perfectly? Not too long. You think your son should go to college to train to become an electrician … wireless electricity is already here and once prices come down, having your house rewired will become a thing of the past.

Manufacturing and production employ 2.25 million in the UK. As mentioned earlier, many of these jobs will soon be automated away. Finally, tourism and hospitality employ 1.4 million people and 2.8 million people work in healthcare.

How will automation impact property and values?

While software that is able to manage your portfolio for you will increase your gross yield, the bigger concern is obviously what will happen to property prices if unemployment rises. Just as the fallout from automation in the industrial sector had a negative impact for a generation in cities like Sheffield, the concern now should be if your property portfolio is located in areas that are known for tertiary employment only. Think about what your tenants do for a job. If they have moved to your area to work at a large shopping centre, hospital, logistical centre or university, then you could see demand fall in your area, both to rent and to buy property.

Yes, I said 'university'! Futurologist Thomas Frey writes on his Futurist Speaker blog[1] that 'by 2030 over 50% of colleges [in the US] will collapse'. Frey says that there are several driving forces that are causing the world of higher education to 'feel the ground shift beneath its feet'.

These include the rising costs of education, with US student loans exceeded $1 trillion for the first time in 2013; the soaring demand for online courses (in less than six years, Apple's iTunes U reached the 1 billion course download threshold, and less than one year after its founding, Coursera had registered 3.2 million students); and finally, the discontent of graduates as 284,000 college graduates in the US were working in minimum-wage jobs in 2012.

Andrew Ng, co-founder of the online education website Coursera, says: 'When one professor can teach 50,000 people, it alters the economics of education.'

This is not just a problem for the developed world either. In China more than 94 million graduates between 2010 and 2020 are expected to be working in blue-collar jobs because of a massive oversupply of talent. According to the *Beijing Times*, China's college graduates on average make only 300

---

[1]   http://www.futuristspeaker.com

yuan, or roughly $44, more per month than the average Chinese migrant worker.

Investment tactics

Obviously in light of the above we need to embrace technological changes, and keeping up-to-date with changes that are without doubt coming our way can only help with your investment decisions. Try browsing futuristic websites like futuretimeline.net, which lists the latest research and the launch date of new tech products.

Investing in companies that create 'life-changing' products will give you great returns in the long run. For example, when Apple launched the iPod in October 2001, its shares were trading at 8.78. By the time it released its second great invention (the iPhone) in June 2007 the share price was 122. By the time Apple released its fourth-generation iPad in November 2012 its share price was 585. That means £10,000 invested in Apple when the iPod was released would be worth £666,000 just 11 years later.

With regard to investing in UK property, I would suggest researching into where the largest IT and R&D companies are or will be located. Employment in the quaternary sector will soar for several decades, and you only have to look at the sharp contrast between property prices in the Silicon Valley in San Francisco and those in bankrupt Detroit to see just what happens if you ignore technology's impact on property prices.

In summary

I would hope that the above has given you some 'food for thought' and will help you to make wiser investing decisions. If you do aspire to become a professionally minded property investor/landlord then you should be reading *Property Investor News* each and every month. The monthly cost is on par with the price of two coffees from Costa Coffee or Starbucks. Can you afford *not* to be informed about the property investing market?

Richard Bowser

Editor of Property Investor News

Property Investor News is the monthly magazine for serious property investors and landlords: www.property-investor-news.com

Simon Zutshi: How to quickly build your cash-generating portfolio of property, using other people's money to replace your income

I first met Sally Lawson back in 2009 when I was invited to speak about successful property investing to a group of her clients. I was really impressed by Sally's proactive approach to being a letting agent, always seeking to give extra value to her clients, for example by putting on quarterly networking events that help them to build their personal contacts and learn more about property investing. This was very smart because Sally understood that if her clients were better educated about property investing they would probably buy more properties, which she, in turn, would then get to manage for them. A true win-win for everyone, and also, I suspect, why she has asked me to write this guest chapter.

If you are reading this book, then I would guess that you are either a letting agent who wants to learn from Sally's vast experience, or a landlord/investor who wants to learn about managing your own property. Either way I believe that you should be buying more property yourself to create extra passive income for yourself, and I am going to explain how you can do that in this chapter.

If you are a letting agent and then become a landlord yourself then you will have a much better understanding of what is important to landlords and so become a more attractive letting agent to other investors.

If you already own some properties you may believe that you are not in a position to purchase any more, if you have run out of deposits. Well, the good news is that in this chapter I am going to briefly explain three concepts which when applied can help you to quickly build a cash-generating portfolio using other people's money. The three concepts are:

1. Five golden rules of property investing

2. Momentum investing to quickly build your portfolio

3. Using other people's money

However, before I start, let me explain about how I started my property journey and one of the biggest revelations I had, which I would like to share with you.

I purchased my first property in 1995, when I started work as a graduate trainee at Cadbury in Birmingham. I rented out two of the rooms in my home to friends who were still at Birmingham University and I found that the rent covered my mortgage and the bills. I pretty much lived for free. This meant I was able to save a lot of my salary and by 1998 I had saved enough money to purchase another property, which I moved into again with some friends who rented rooms from me. I kept the first property, which has been rented to students ever since.

Over the next three years I purchased a few more properties and flipped a few, until I got to the point toward the end of 2000 when my accountant informed me that I had made more money from my property part-time than I had as a full-time senior manager at Cadbury. In 2001 I was able to leave my corporate job and by 2003 I had completely replaced my former salary with income from property. However, this is when I had a lightbulb moment that I want to share with you.

I had started to manage my properties, all of which were within five minutes' drive of where I lived in Birmingham. I found that managing a few properties did not take too much time and I actually enjoyed it. To be honest I thought that I could do a better job than most agents and I did not want to give a letting agent 10% of my rental income. If you are a landlord then I am sure that you have felt this way as well in the past.

This was all fine until I fell into what I call the landlord trap. Managing a few properties was not very time-consuming but I found that the more properties I owned, the more time I had to spend looking after them, which meant that I had less time to focus on buying them and my acquisition rate dramatically slowed. I was making good income from my property but it was far from passive, as I had become a full-time property manager. I realised that I had swapped my job at Cadbury, which I had really enjoyed, for a job as a property manager, which I was not passionate about. This was ironic as the whole point of my investing in property was to give me a passive income so that I was free to do the things I wanted to do.

This is when I decided to hand over all of the management of my properties to a good letting agent. It meant that I took a short-term dip in income but I was able to get all of my time back. I was then able to concentrate on buying property and thus quickly replaced the income shortfall and in fact far exceeded my former corporate salary.

I understand the desire to manage your first few properties but, believe me, the novelty soon wears off. I encourage all of my students to make sure that they account for the cost of someone else managing their property when they do the calculation to assess if they should purchase a property or not. You can still manage your property if you really want to, but that is not why most people get into property investing in my experience.

The challenge can be in finding a good letting agent, like Sally, who really knows what they are doing and will look after your property and your tenants for you. I find the best way to do this is through word-of-mouth recommendation. Ask other investors in your area who they use and what their experience is of that agent.

A great place to meet other investors and letting agents is at property networking meetings. If you look in the back of this book, there are details of how you can attend one of the property investor network meetings (which is normally £20) courtesy of Sally Lawson.

So let's focus on the three elements that I want to cover in this chapter.

The Five Golden Rules of Property Investing

Investing in property is a bit like buying yourself a cash machine that gives you money every month. The idea is that you find a property which you can easily rent out and where after deducting all of the costs, such as the mortgage, insurance, maintenance, letting agents' fees etc., there is some profit left over for you each month. Sounds straightforward, right? Well, yes, it is, but you do need to know what you are doing to avoid the costly mistakes that most investors make.

When I wrote my first book, *Property Magic*, back in 2008, I wanted to create some rules which investors could follow to minimise the risk of investing and maximise their return. The result was these five golden rules, which I would like to briefly share with you.

1. Always buy from motivated sellers.

Instead of looking for a property you like and then negotiating with the seller, a smarter strategy is to look for motivated sellers who will be flexible on the price and/or the terms of the sale, and then decide if you want to buy that particular property. The amount of discount will vary depending on the motivation of the seller and the general market conditions. In a rising market you may be happy with a 15% to 20% discount. In a falling market you would want a bigger discount of 25% to 40% to give you more of a safety buffer in case prices come down further.

2. Buy in an area with strong rental demand.

This is more important than getting a discount! Remember you don't want to be paying for the mortgage on your rental property. That is what you have tenants for. You must make sure there is good rental demand in the area so that if your tenants ever leave, you can quickly find new tenants at the full market rent.

3. Buy for cash flow.

Your property should create a monthly positive cash flow for you so that it is an asset rather than a liability. Although we expect property prices to rise in the long term, if you buy your investments 'as if prices will never go up again' you will be forced to only buy properties which give you great cash flow now. Extra cash flow will help you to build up a cash safety buffer, and will help you cover potential rises in interest rates in the future.

4. Invest for the long term; buy and hold.

Some investors buy and sell property to make a profit. The real profit, however, is in buying and holding for the long term to benefit from significant capital growth. If you plan to hold for the long term and your property is rented out, creating a positive cash flow, you do not mind short-term fluctuations in price.

5. Have a cash buffer.

The investors who get into difficulty are often the ones who do not have any spare cash to access in case of an emergency. As an investor, you will incur unexpected costs and so you must have some spare cash to cover these instances. The size of this buffer depends on your personal level of risk.

Momentum investing to quickly build your portfolio

The more of these profitable cash machines that you have in your portfolio, the sooner you can replace your income. A common problem that many investors experience is that they run out of deposit money. The traditional way to grow your portfolio is to wait for the property values and the rents to go up and then remortgage your property to pull out some equity, which can then be used as a deposit to buy the next property. The obvious problem is that you have to wait for several years for the market to increase enough to be able to remortgage.

With the use of momentum investing you can recycle your deposit every six to nine months and so build your portfolio much quicker. Here is how it works:

We find a motivated seller who has a property worth £120k that we can buy for £90k, which is 25% below market value. Before I go any further, I know that some readers may struggle to understand why, or even to believe that someone would sell at this low price. The fact is that for some motivated sellers the speed and certainty of the sale is more important than the amount of money they receive. You have to learn how to find these people but they are out there, no matter what is happening in the property market.

So back to the example. Although the value is £120k, you have agreed to purchase at the discounted price of £90k. You would need to put down the normal 25% deposit, which in this case is £22,500, and you get a buy-to-let mortgage for £67,500. In the UK, most mortgage lenders will require you to hold a property for six months before you remortgage it. After you have owned it for six months you can apply for a remortgage based on the true value of £120k, which means that you should be able to remortgage it to £90k. This means that once you have paid off the first mortgage the money left over is your original deposit, which comes back to you so that you can use it on your next purchase.

The main problem is that you tie up your deposit for six months until you can remortgage the property and you also have increased costs due to having two surveys, two sets of legal costs and potentially two arrangement fees on the finance.

Another potential issue when you come to remortgage is that you may struggle to prove the true value at £120k if you originally purchased it just six months previously for £90k. To overcome this it can be useful to obtain an independent RICS (Royal Institute of Chartered Surveyors) valuation *before* you purchase it to show the true value of £120k, and take some pictures before and after any work you do to demonstrate that you have added value.

Using other people's money

No matter how much money you have or don't have, at some point everyone runs out of their own funds. At this point you have two choices. You either stop buying property, or you find an alternative way to fund deposits. All of the really successful investors that I know have used their own and other people's money to build their portfolio.

As a nation we don't like talking about money and the thought of approaching family and friends to ask them for money is not very appealing to most people. Whilst I completely understand this, it all comes down to the way you do it and what you are offering. Instead of asking people to lend money, you could ask them if they know anyone who might like to get a great return on their money. This is a much easier question to ask and takes the pressure off you and the other person. They may well know someone who might be interested or may say that they themselves would like to know more.

With interest rates at a record low, anyone who has money in the bank is not really earning any money, especially when you take the current level of inflation into account. As long as you have a great property deal you can offer someone a rate much higher than they are currently getting in the bank. If you use momentum investing as described already in this chapter, you can borrow the money for a short amount of time and then return it to them and you are left with the property with equity and cash flow.

You may find a property where you can't use momentum investing and you need to leave the money in, but which has a very high rental return, such as a multi-let property let out on a room-by-room basis to young professionals. With this type of property and tenant, there may be sufficient income to cover all of the costs, pay the investor a good return on their money, and still have enough cash left over to give you some profit each month.

You may not think or believe that anyone would lend you money, even if they had it to lend. However, you would be surprised at how many people do have money sitting in their bank, which right now is not doing anything for them because the interest rates are so low. They may be very happy to help you if they also see the benefit for them.

The caveat to all of this is that when dealing with other people's money you must make sure you know what you are doing to ensure that you can give the money back to them at the agreed time with the agreed amount of interest.

The best thing for you to do is to educate yourself as to how to find these great deals. Once you have great deals there will be no shortage of people who will want to work with you to get a better return on their money. A great place to find people like this is at property network meetings where people go to further their knowledge, mix with like-minded positive people and find potential joint venture partners who they can work with. In the back of this book there are details of how you can attend your first pin meeting for free as Sally's guest as a thank-you for buying this book.

I do hope this chapter has got you thinking of how you could increase your portfolio to give you more income. Now is a great time to invest. By educating yourself you can learn how to minimise the risks and maximise your return. I wish you the best of luck on your property investing journey, and remember it is much easier and more fun to do it with other people than to try to do it on your own, which can be a lonely journey.

Very best wishes,

Simon Zutshi
Founder of property investors network

Simon Zutshi is the author of the property investing bestseller Property Magic, and one of the top property investment speakers, trainers and mentors in the UK. He pioneered property networking in the UK when he founded the property investors network in 2003, which has grown to become the largest and fastest-growing organisation for property investors and professionals with 50+ evening networking meetings each month all around the UK. In 2014 Simon set up www.CrowdProperty.com, a new peer-to-peer lending platform specifically for the property industry.

Concentric® ((C
SALES & LETTINGS
The Property Experts

Working FOR yourself but not BY yourself

With our emphasis on training and support, you too could be earning £35,000 per month income within 3 years by taking on a franchise with us. We help you become a 'property expert' in your area, to work with landlords to help them buy, let and manage rental property profitably and safely.

Create the life, build the income & live the dream

Visit us on:

www.concentric-franchise.co.uk

Welcome to a **bright**, new **world**

for **Letting Agents**

"*I'm Hannah and I'm confident that our unique specialist solutions let you offer an unbeatable proposition to landlords, managing their risk and optimising rental yield*"

Are you interested in benefiting from the rising UK property market?

"Investing in property gives an investor both asset and income, but buying right is essential. The property investors network supports its delegates by teaching them all the essential areas of property investment, so that they can achieve their own property success"

Sally Lawson

Since 2003, the property investors network (pin) have provided a friendly, supportive and positive environment for you to become a more successful investor. They don't sell property, just teach you how to be a successful investor.

There are now 50 monthly meetings all around the UK so there is bound to be a meeting close to where you live or work.

Here's how you can benefit by attending your local pin meeting:

- Keep up to date with the changes in the market
- Learn the latest investing strategies
- Mix with other like-minded successful people
- Learn from other investors' mistakes
- Be inspired by other investors' achievements
- Build your personal network of property contacts

Attend a pin meeting courtesy of Sally for FREE!

Entry to pin is normally £20; however, if it is your first meeting, you can attend as Sally's guest for free. Or indeed if you know of someone that has not yet been to a pin meeting, just give them the special voucher code and easy-to-follow steps below.

To take up this offer all you need to do is:

- Go to **http://www.pinmeeting.co.uk**
- Select which pin meeting you would like to attend
- Click "**Book using a voucher code**"
- Enter your contact details
- Enter "**Tenant**" into the voucher code box - Click **Apply voucher**
- Click "**Click Here to book your place now**"
- An email confirmation will be sent to you

Visit the website now: www.PinMeeting.co.uk

Make sure that you make the most of the rising UK property market and the incredible investment opportunities available now!

pin
property
investors
network